Capital Contest

Deepak Bajpai, a former investigative journalist, left NDTV to volunteer and then joined the Aam Aadmi Party (AAP). A former National Treasurer and Secretary of Arvind Kejriwal's political secretariat, and a member of the Political Affairs Committee, the party's highest decision-making body, Bajpai has worked closely with the top leadership as well as volunteers of the party. An intrinsic part of the core AAP team, he has been actively involved in the party's strategic choices, which puts him in a unique position to bring out the insights of this crucial election and the AAP's evolution.

Sidharth Pandey, an award-winning journalist with more than two decades of experience, has been keenly tracking the growth of the AAP from long before the party was even formed. Having worked closely on the Right to Information (RTI) Act, on which both Arvind Kejriwal and Manish Sisodia had started their social movements during their pre-AAP days, Pandey helps weave a narrative as an independent observer of the evolution of AAP's key leaders and the party itself.

Capital Contest

HOW AAP AND KEJRIWAL WON DELHI

DEEPAK BAJPAI *and*
SIDHARTH PANDEY

RUPA

Published by
Rupa Publications India Pvt. Ltd 2020
7/16, Ansari Road, Daryaganj
New Delhi 110002

Sales centres:
Allahabad Bengaluru Chennai
Hyderabad Jaipur Kathmandu
Kolkata Mumbai

ISBN: 978-93-90356-20-1

First impression 2020

10 9 8 7 6 5 4 3 2 1

The moral right of the authors has been asserted.

Printed at HT Media Ltd, Gr. Noida

CONTENTS

PREFACE

Battleground Delhi: Round Two

Delhi, the capital of India. With more than 19 million (1.9 crore) people, it is among the world's most populous agglomerations. Delhi's population is more than that of 10 other Indian states, including Uttarakhand, Arunachal Pradesh and Tripura. By 2028, Delhi is set to become the most populous city on earth, according to the United Nations (UN). So, the city/state of Delhi is neither small geographically, nor insignificant numerically.

The political fortunes of the capital always weigh much heavier than its size. What happened in the capital in the 2020 assembly elections is the story of the Aam Aadmi Party's (AAP) victory, and it is a story that needs to be told because it is a rare and momentous milestone in the political history of the nation.

While AAP's 2013 assembly victory had taken by surprise a nation beleaguered by charges of corruption and the seeming power of privilege of the Congress party that had been ruling for too many years, it is AAP's victory in the 2020 assembly elections that needs to be studied more closely. The 2020 Delhi elections were one of the most bitterly fought elections in recent times with the chief minister (CM), Arvind Kejriwal, who had called himself an 'anarchist' many years ago, being labelled by the central government leaders as a 'terrorist' and accused of buying voters.

By this time, the AAP had been in power for a full five-year term and the 2020 elections came on the back of a crushing defeat for the AAP by the Bharatiya Janata Party (BJP) in the 2019 national elections.[1] The challenger, Prime Minister (PM) Narendra Modi and his juggernaut, were unstoppable. The BJP was taking this battle against the AAP, head-on. The BJP and PM Modi had much to reach out to the public with. The PM stood tall with numerous wins under his belt—public acclaim for the Balakot surgical strike against terror camps in Pakistan; the Supreme Court's landmark verdict allowing the Ram Mandir to be built where there used to be a masjid, thus meeting the aspirations of the majority of Hindus in India; a following from the hundreds of thousands of majoritarians, convinced that the only future for the country was with the BJP and that the party would bring back the glory of the Hindutva way of life. In such an atmosphere, it was as if there was not the slightest space for anyone else to even try to take a shot at any level of leadership. The 2020 Delhi elections were close on the heels of a very communalized situation surrounding protests against the controversial Citizenship (Amendment) Act (CAA). Long before election day 2020, several media commentators and strategists had already called the battle for Delhi as won and lost.

And yet, as journalists, we had personally witnessed the birth of the most improbable government in Delhi, a government made of maverick do-gooders, most with zero experience in either politics or governance at a national level,

---

[1]The AAP was decimated in the Lok Sabha polls of 2019. Unlike in 2014, in 2019, its Lok Sabha seats were reduced from an earlier four to just one. It lost all the seven Lok Sabha seats of Delhi and hence, a crushing defeat in the Lok Sabha.

for a country the scale of India! What they lacked in experience, they made up for with passion and enthusiasm, often leaving a trail of chaos behind. But by 2019, the AAP, with a little over five years of having been at the helm of affairs, had gained some maturity through its experience of having learnt in the actual doing.

The party was striving to reach out to the people of Delhi and to meet their aspirations. Their leader Kejriwal was a man who prided himself on an equal mix of integrity and a belief in playing Superman to ensure that his government delivered what it had promised. In many ways, his government was going to be different, both from those that had gone before him, and from those who were his contemporaries in other states.

In this book, we meet the key players in CM Kejriwal's team, who tell us how they went from victory to despair and back to victory again. They have been the key architects of the party and its victory.

As journalists, we have reported on what the AAP was claiming it had done for the people of Delhi. Like them, we were surprised by the real results in the community. The mohalla clinics gave people a chance to get a check-up closer home, without waiting hopelessly in long queues at Delhi's prestigious government hospitals, such as the All India Institute of Medical Sciences (AIIMS). The clinics, used by a million people in the first couple of years, provide a first line of treatment, which often eliminates the need for further treatment. The government schools were upgraded to match private schools in curricula and in creature comforts, and boasted brightly lit and colourfully painted classrooms. The teachers are actually striving to provide quality education in government schools and are available and answerable to parents to talk about the progress of children.

In 2019, the AAP launched its high-voltage election promise, announcing free power for consumers. The criterion for getting a waiver on the monthly bill was that the consumer used less than 200 units of power a month. Those who criticized this 'freebie' were reminded that these 200 units were nothing compared to a Member of Parliament (MP) getting 4,000 units of electricity free of charge.

That this election was won, despite the entire might of the BJP government holding rallies and doing door-to-door campaigning, coupled with the availability of enormous amounts of funds and hence, the ability to buy much media time and space, was amazing. Despite all this, David did beat Goliath, hands down, because people were actually weighing who was serving the best interests of the public and the answer was the AAP.

When Deepak discussed with me the co-authoring of a book on this victory, I was very excited, as this story had to be told and the backstories of the key team members shared. My association with Kejriwal goes back in time to 2005, when he worked in Delhi on the Right to Information (RTI) Act. I have always respected what he has stood for and what he had achieved through these years.

However, soon after we started mapping the contours of this book with the publisher, the COVID-19 situation began to get out of hand, and when by midnight of 24 March the first lockdown came into effect, we were still listing the chapters. So, this book is an achievement of several interviews done face to face before the lockdown and many online interviews, meetings, research and everything else. Of course, by the time we were writing the last chapter, several of the key persona who had to be interviewed, such as Kejriwal and Manish Sisodia, were personally totally involved in leading the battle against coronavirus in the capital, and their planned interviews had to be put on the back-burner several times, before we could finally talk to them about their vision for the future.

However, we feel that with this book, we bring you closer to several key players in the party who have shared their experiences and provide fresh insights on how the small, 'new-kid-on-the-block' party pulled the punches and how, after the opportunity of serving their constituents for a full five-year term, their experience brought political and administrative maturity.

We meet the management consultant and entrepreneur-turned-AAP political campaigner Kapil Bhardwaj, who is a 12th-generation Dilliwallah. He ensured that despite the 2019 loss, the party quickly geared up and was ready to take on the battle for AAP's survival. The only way forward was to listen up: to listen to the volunteers, to the experts and political observers and, most importantly, to the voters. AAP's very existence depended on the 2020 assembly elections.

So what were the lessons from the 2019 Lok Sabha polls? Was AAP's message not getting through to the voters? These answers were vital for the AAP and for Jasmine Shah, who was to be the primary lead for the party's media campaign in the 2020 Delhi elections; this programme was going to be an eye-opener and it was crucial to get the party's messaging right. A three-pronged approach was followed, which was crucial if the AAP wanted to get back into the fighting ring.

One of the things which emerged was that 'the expectations from the AAP are immense. We are a political disruptor. We keep saying that we are not here for the power and it's our ideology for clean and effective governance which drives us, but at the same time, if we don't win, then it will be said that it is our ideology that has failed,' said Preeti Sharma Menon, spokesperson and National Executive member of the AAP.

Menon says, 'Almost all the people who have joined our party have done so because they want to bring about a change in politics. There must be the romance of belief, but we needed to ensure both for our voters as well as for our volunteers, that we deliver on the promises we had made.'

Romance may have swayed the voters in 2015, but it was Satyendra Jain, architect-turned-politician and one of Kejriwal's most trusted aides and versatile Cabinet ministers, who came up with what several believe to be the game changer for the AAP in the 2020 Delhi elections. Working closely with Kejriwal, he suggested the free electricity package, and worked closely with the team to ensure delivery of other benefits such as mohalla clinics, free bus travel for women and many other schemes that became important to the people of Delhi.

The AAP was outflanked and outspent by the BJP, which had deployed its line-up of central ministers, MPs and CMs from other states to campaign for Delhi 2020. In such a situation, Ankit Lal and his team successfully used social media to amplify the party's message and also challenge the BJP. Lal has handled social media for all the elections since the inception of the AAP. Following the stunning victory of the BJP in Uttar Pradesh (UP), where a powerful WhatsApp network had played a key role, the AAP decided to learn from the winners.

The AAP effectively used social media to connect volunteers with office-bearers; it created Vidhan Sabha-wise WhatsApp groups of volunteers to quickly disseminate information and during the 2020 assembly elections, it successfully used these channels to counter propaganda pushed by its opponents. Before electioneering started, AAP's WhatsApp warriors were ready under Lal.

Elections also need money and that's where Pankaj Gupta and Neeraj Gulati, both highly successful entrepreneurs and troubleshooters for the AAP, came in as key fundraisers.

For the 2013 elections, Kejriwal made an emotional appeal to Delhiites that he needed ₹20 crore to fight the elections, as the party had no money. People were surprised and said that if a politician was asking for money, then the party could not be corrupt. By going out and seeking donations, the AAP seemed to be only reinforcing that image.

As donations started pouring in, the party website kept track of the donations and displayed the total payments received at any given point. The moment it crossed the benchmark of ₹20 crore, the website stopped accepting donations. Kejriwal went a step further. On the morning of 17 November 2013, he tweeted: 'Our party needed ₹20 crores to fight elections. We have met the target. We don't need any more money for Delhi elections.'

If the 2015 Delhi elections were unprecedented with the AAP winning 67 of the 70 seats in the capital, 2020 was remarkable given the fact that the BJP's election machinery had put in all its might into the contest.

Professor Abhay Kumar Dubey, political commentator, feels that what cost the BJP a victory in the 2020 Delhi assembly elections was the use of two different models of development. The Modi model, used countrywide by the BJP in the lead-up to the 2019 national elections, targeted the poorest of the poor and the marginalized to deliver free gas, zero-balance bank accounts and health insurance coverage of up to ₹5 lakh, and so in the process, netted 10 crore additional voters. This model did not work in Delhi as the immigrant worker, though poor, earned just enough to be cut off from receiving these benefits. The AAP model, on the other hand, carefully studied the needs of the Delhi voter and, for five years, worked to give them the things they needed most: free electricity of up to 200 units, free water, free bus rides for women, good mohalla clinics and government schools which are now the envy of many private schools.

Sisodia, Deputy CM and the right-hand man of Kejriwal, talks about listening to the citizens of Delhi and understanding their needs and honestly addressing these. He says that it is the job of the government to instill a sense of confidence in the mind and heart of the common man of Delhi. If a child is born in the family, the parents don't need to worry about providing the child with quality education and the child needn't worry about providing affordable and quality healthcare for the ageing parents. The AAP has been working towards this and this is why the people voted for their party.

So, where does the AAP go from here? How does it plan on expanding? Aatishi Singh, an academic-turned-politician and one of the main strategists for the party, shares her candid thoughts on the way forward for the AAP. Singh articulates her vision for the country and for AAP's important role in the future of the country. 'Some fights are not fought only when you are assured of the victory. They are fought because that's the right thing to do. And that's what we did. And we will do it over and over again.'

Singh feels that the current national political disposition is fuelling a public debate on the basis of hate and divisiveness. Hence, it is all the more important for parties such as the AAP to ensure a future based on development—one aimed at meeting the needs of the ordinary citizen. And this should be accomplished on the basis of cohesiveness and love. She adds, 'In some sense, we are now a different party. Back then, we talked of a dream—a dream of corruption-free governance, a dream of functional public schools and hospitals, and people-centric governance. We have proved that the dream is a possibility, and in fact, a reality. And now we are saying all of India can be very different. We can all live in a healthy, educated, peaceful and loving country. The only change needed is in its politics.'

The architect of it all, the Delhi CM describes the 2020 Delhi elections as a major turning point in politics. 'Decades-old identity and formula politics of divide and rule can be decisively defeated and buried through people-centric politics of development. This was the clear message from the 2020 elections,' says Kejriwal.

Kejriwal says that the message of the 2020 Delhi elections is particularly important for the youth of this country and 'it has inspired millions of youth who aspire to bring about change, who want to serve their country.' He adds, 'In less than 24 hours of the announcement of the Delhi election results, more than 11 lakh people registered with the AAP to join its mission to transform our country. Most of them are young people from UP, Bihar, Punjab, Maharashtra and other states.'

Bringing the story of the 2020 Delhi assembly elections, *Capital Contest* is an essential read not only for those who keenly track politics and sociology, but for all those who are interested in understanding how India has and continues to change and how its politicians must continuously monitor the pulse of the people so as to be in sync with a fast-changing nation.

�❧

1

DECIMATION

'*Hamari charo taraf se pitayi ho rahi thi* (We were being defeated from all sides)', Kapil Bhardwaj tells us. Counting of votes for the 2019 Lok Sabha elections had begun barely two hours ago and these were just the early trends, yet Bhardwaj, who was AAP's operations and organization manager, knew it was all over for the AAP.

To all who know him, Bhardwaj is one of the most optimistic persons in the team, the kind who is capable of making lemonade from the lemons handed by life. However, this was not one of those times.

It wasn't that Bhardwaj and hundreds of volunteers under him hadn't tried. They, along with the party's top leadership, had been careful to avoid some of the past mistakes. This time, the party had avoided spreading itself too thin as it had in the 2014 Lok Sabha polls, when it had contested 432 seats in all 29 states of India. The fact that it had managed to win just four seats in the 2014 elections was an important lesson to remember. In the 2019 Lok Sabha polls, the party narrowed its campaign to just 33 candidates in Delhi, Goa, Punjab, Chandigarh, Haryana, Bihar, UP, and Andaman and Nicobar. But despite that, the AAP was looking at decimation across the country. Before the day was over, the party had managed to win just one seat, which was worse than its 2014 performance.

Ironically, apart from Delhi, the AAP had been banking on Punjab to send its candidates to Parliament. The party had drawn strength from the experience of the 2017 state elections, where it won 20 of the 117 seats, relegating the Shiromani Akali Dal (SAD) to the third place. While Captain Amarinder Singh and the Congress won a comfortable majority with 77 of the 117 seats, having edged out the SAD, the AAP was given the position of the Leader of the Opposition.

During the 2019 Lok Sabha polls, however, even Punjab had let down the AAP, like the rest of the country. While in the 2014 Lok Sabha elections, it had won all the four seats that it contested from Punjab, five years later, it managed to hold onto only one seat, losing the three others. The only saving grace came from sitting MP and popular actor and comedy artist Bhagwant Singh Mann, who managed to retain his seat from Sangrur, Punjab.

If the Lok Sabha elections in Punjab was a disappointment, Delhi was a decimation for the party. It not only failed to win any of the seven seats in Delhi, it slid to the third position behind the Congress in all except South and North-west Delhi, where it secured second position to the BJP. In the 2014 Lok Sabha elections, the AAP had been in the second position in all seven constituencies. This came as a big blow to the AAP. For Bhardwaj, who was in charge of the West Delhi Lok Sabha seat, the defeat seemed more personal.

The management consultant and entrepreneur-turned-political campaigner, Bhardwaj is a 12th-generation Dilliwallah. He admits that while winning Delhi may have seemed tough in the national election, he had never imagined that the party would not win even a few of the assembly segments which form a Parliamentary seat in Delhi. That even the Congress had managed to perform better than the AAP in Delhi was certainly a cause of worry.

'The fact that at the national level, there was no clear contender to take on Narendra Modi gave the BJP a clear advantage with voters; however, the fact that the Congress was the voters' second choice was a major point of disappointment and worry for us,' admits Bhardwaj.

As AAP's chief opposition tracker, Bhardwaj says that he personally visited 117 polling centres and realized that it was going to be a tough battle for the party in Delhi, but even then he had never imagined that it would be a complete wipeout for them.

'When voters come to the stations set up by political parties near polling booths, you can tell which way they are voting. It's the way they look at you. Even by not saying whom they are planning to vote for, there are always clear indications of who they are going to vote for,' says Bhardwaj.

Interestingly, the AAP had launched its door-to-door campaigning for the Lok Sabha polls in Delhi in October 2018, more than four months before election dates were announced by the Election Commission of India (ECI) on 10 March 2019. They planned to deploy a team of 3,000 volunteers to go to each and every house and campaign for the party. The plan was for the volunteers to do one quick round with all the voters, informing them about the schemes launched by the AAP.

'The BJP is a well-oiled election machine and that's what we were fighting against,' says Bhardwaj. 'For every rupee we were putting in advertising and communication, the BJP was deploying 300 times that,' he explains. What it could not match in terms of resources, the AAP had hoped to make up for by starting its campaign early and covering more ground than the BJP.

The other disadvantage that the AAP had was that it was playing on BJP's turf at the national level. Modi was already an established and proven leader and star campaigner for his party. So much so that the BJP's main campaign slogan was *'Modi hai toh mumkin hai* (If there's Modi, it's possible)'. Like 2014, the BJP had once again turned the Lok Sabha elections into a sort of Presidential contest as in the United States (US), where contenders from the Democrat and Republican parties end up facing off against each other. While the BJP was projecting Modi as the reason why voters should opt for the party, Kejriwal made 'Poorna Rajya' or 'full statehood' for Delhi the main election plank for his party.

'This was a national election and we realized that people were going to vote on national issues. For us, the most important issue was improving the governance in Delhi and for this, getting full statehood was critical,' says Bhardwaj.

Till 1991, Delhi had been a Union Territory, which meant that it was directly administered by the Centre. That was until the Parliament, in 1991, voted to give Delhi special status by the 69th Amendment of the Constitution. Delhi came to be formally called the National Capital Territory of Delhi. While the amendment created a state legislative assembly and certain powers were accorded to it, several other powers such as law and order, including control of the police and land, continued to be with the Centre. This has been one of the main points of contention between the AAP and the central government, with the former insisting that the police should be under the control of the directly elected government.

With more than 19 million (1.9 crore) people, Delhi's population is more than that of 10 other states, including

Uttarakhand, Arunachal Pradesh and Tripura. India's capital city is also the world's second-most populous urban agglomeration and by 2028 is set to become the most populous city on earth, according to the UN—a huge population with equally big and rising aspirations which, according to the AAP, cannot be fully met unless the Delhi government is given similar rights as other state governments, including control of the police.

Interestingly, both the Congress and the BJP had raised the demand for full statehood for Delhi in the past. However, the AAP accuses both its rivals of only using it as a political gimmick. According to Bhardwaj, 'If the BJP and the Congress really wanted to give Delhi greater powers and full statehood, then it could have been done by both in the past when both parties have had the same political party or group in control of the government in the Centre and in Delhi.'

'I cannot even transfer a peon without a nod from the Centre,' Delhi CM Kejriwal had famously claimed in a press conference in February 2019. The press conference was prompted by an important judgement from the Supreme Court of India on 14 February 2019.[1] Dissatisfied with the Delhi High Court's ruling in the matter, the Delhi government had taken the case to the Supreme Court. It wanted the apex court to finally decide who controlled what: what were the limits of powers between the Delhi government and the central government? Unfortunately for the Delhi government, the two judges of the Supreme Court who had heard the case ruled that the present arrangement under the Constitution gave the Centre the final say over the postings and transfer of bureaucrats in Delhi. The judges were, however, split over

---

[1] Govt of NCT of Delhi v. Union of India, 2019 SCC OnLine SC 193.

the question of delivery of services and, as a result, a larger bench of the court will have to decide on the matter.

The AAP was also hoping that the apex court would restore control of the Anti-Corruption Bureau (ACB), the department that investigates cases of corruption, to the state government. However, here, too, the court ruled that it was the Centre and not the state government that had control over the bureau. The tussle over the ACB had become a sore point between the Kejriwal government and the Centre, with the former accusing the latter of deliberately stalling investigations into cases of corruption and cronyism.

The AAP had been hoping to get back control of the ACB, which had seen a surge in several cases registered in 2015 against even central government public servants under Kejriwal as CM. While the Delhi Police was still out of the hands of the Delhi government, it was using the ACB to act. However, in May 2015, the Centre issued a notification, which while reinforcing an earlier 1993 order by the Centre, barred the ACB from making a case 'against officers, employees and functionaries of the Central Government.'[2]

To underscore the importance of the ACB to the AAP, Bhardwaj talks about his growing-up years. 'My father used to be in the Municipal Corporation of Delhi (which was subsequently divided into two smaller corporations). He was an engineer for over 22 years and he used to often tell me that when it comes to corruption, the "big fish" always managed to escape and it's only the "small fish" that ever got trapped.'

'You see, corruption is there in the US also, but unlike India, they make sure that they catch the big fish to set an

---

[2]*The Gazette of India: Extraordinary*. Available at: https://www.mha.gov.in/sites/default/files/video_87.pdf, last accessed on 29 June 2020.

example. They use the small fish to catch the big one. That is what Kejriwal was trying to do when the bureau was snatched away from him,' says Bhardwaj.

It was against this backdrop and the ongoing tussle between the Delhi government and the Centre, that Kejriwal made 'full statehood' for Delhi his party's main electoral issue in the 2019 Lok Sabha elections and asked citizens of Delhi to elect all seven AAP candidates.

The problem for the AAP was that voters still saw the 2019 elections as a national election. With the AAP nowhere close to offering an alternative to the BJP or other larger parties at the national level, it was simply not in the running.

'Many voters also told us that even if we were to elect the AAP to all of Delhi's seven seats, how could it achieve its goal of statehood for Delhi when others had failed to do so? Voters were simply not convinced or impressed enough to vote for the AAP in the Lok Sabha polls in Delhi,' says Bhardwaj.

Flirting with the Congress

Sensing that the fight was going to be a tough one, Kejriwal sent out feelers to the Congress for a possible tie-up in Delhi ahead of the 2019 polls. It's no secret that the BJP has historically done well whenever there was a triangular contest or where there are more opponents to split the vote. The grand old party of India, which had been wiped out in the 2015 assembly elections in Delhi after it failed to win even one seat, had improved its performance in the 2017 municipal elections in the capital, where it had seen a jump in its vote share. In that same election, while the BJP won most of the seats, the cumulative vote share of the Congress and the AAP was 47 per cent, better than the 36 per cent of the BJP. In the 2014

Lok Sabha polls, while the BJP had won all of Delhi's seven seats, the AAP and the Congress had a vote share higher than the BJP's in six of the seven parliamentary seats.

Almost two years later, the Congress was rising from the ashes. The AAP needed to make a statement that it was a serious player and an alliance with the Congress could have been the way forward. The two parties had a history of a bad marriage in 2014. Barely three months before that parting, the AAP had made its debut in Delhi, winning 28 of the 70 seats. When the BJP fell short of forming a government on its own, it decided to not make a bid for government formation. With no one in a position to form the government by themselves, the Congress decided to extend 'conditional outside support' to the AAP and Kejriwal was sworn in as the CM on 28 December 2013, thus becoming the second-youngest CM of Delhi. (Chaudhary Brahm Prakash Yadav was the first and youngest CM of Delhi from 1952 to 1955.) However, the marriage between the two parties was short-lived. Forty-nine days later, Kejriwal and his Cabinet resigned. Kejriwal claimed that both the BJP and the Congress were stonewalling AAP's key legislation on the Lokpal law, a key anti-graft measure, and his party had no option but to resign and seek a fresh mandate. This eventually forced fresh elections in Delhi, with the AAP coming back to power with a brute majority.

In 2019, the Congress understandably was wary of AAP's advances. There had been several rounds of secret talks between both parties and it seemed that a deal could be clinched to mount a real challenge to the BJP in Delhi. The main stumbling block was the seat-sharing formula. The AAP was insisting on contesting six seats in Delhi while giving one to the Congress. It also wanted four in Punjab and one in Chandigarh. The Congress wanted to contest three seats each with the AAP in

Delhi, leaving the seventh seat to an 'eminent person'. With no breakthrough over seat-sharing, the Congress finally pulled the plug. Three-time Delhi CM and senior Congress leader, Sheila Dikshit, ended the speculation by announcing that the Congress had 'unanimously decided' not to have an alliance with the AAP.

Kejriwal also hit back, accusing the Congress of helping the BJP by splitting the anti-BJP vote. While a failure to reach an agreement over seat-sharing was the main reason, several Congressmen had been wary of an understanding with the AAP given past experience. Another reason why the Congress was wary was because of the upcoming state assembly polls in less than six months. The AAP had grown through the fall of the Congress and so, an alliance with the AAP would not help the Congress in the state polls, especially if the party felt it was on an upsurge.

The BJP was happy that that the 2020 Delhi elections were going to be a triangular contest after all, with both the AAP and the Congress deciding to go their own way. A confident party chief, Manoj Tiwari even wished Kejriwal, 'Get well, Mr Kejriwal. The Congress also knows that the BJP will win hands down, alliance or not.'

The party had faced its worst-ever defeat in Delhi in the Lok Sabha polls, just eight months before the Delhi assembly elections. AAP's very existence depended on the 2020 assembly elections. It had to quickly move from licking its wounds of the Lok Sabha polls and prepare for an election that would not only decide its future, but also whether or not it would remain a political force in Delhi. There was talk among party leaders on whether the AAP would become like the Asom Gana Parishad (AGP). The AGP had grabbed the attention of voters and won the Assam state elections, installing Prafulla

Kumar Mahanta as the youngest CM of the state in 1996. Today, however, the party is a pale shadow of its earlier avatar, as it suffers from internal bickering and Mahanta himself is seemingly on the fringes of his party. Was this story going to repeat itself with the AAP? Looking at the party's performance in the Lok Sabha elections, the mainstream media and political pundits were already writing its obituary.

The Lok Sabha results were devastating. It is not just that the party had lost all seven seats to the BJP, what turned it into an existential crisis was the fact that the party had secured only 18.1 per cent of votes to emerge third in the race. The Congress, which was the runner-up, had secured 22.5 per cent votes, giving its best performance since losing power in Delhi at the end of 2013. The BJP, with 56.5 per cent votes, had the highest vote share secured by any party ever, and was smelling blood.

Delhi was the epicentre of the movement which gave birth to the AAP. It had secured a vote share of 29.5 per cent in the 2013 elections, when it was less than a year old. In the 2015 assembly elections, when Kejriwal and his team stunned political observers by winning 67 of 70 seats, the party had secured 54 per cent of votes. Even at the lowest point of its popularity, the party had mopped up 26 per cent of votes in the 2017 Municipal Corporation of Delhi (MCD) elections. But the performance in the 2019 Lok Sabha elections had broken all records. The booth-wise analysis revealed that the AAP had been robbed of its core vote bank's loyalty. Unauthorized colonies, minority and Poorvanchali pockets, and Dalit pockets seemed to have voted against Kejriwal. This had not only shaken the party's confidence, but had also thrown out of the window the very factors on which the party had based its electoral calculations. The party leadership did not know which pocket to call its stronghold any more. It did know where to start for the decisive battle for Delhi, which was just eight months away.

Two MLAs had crossed over to the BJP during the Lok Sabha elections and BJP leaders were openly saying that 14 more MLAs were in touch with them, waiting to switch sides. The Congress also seemed to have renewed vigour and was ready to give a good fight to the AAP. Kejriwal knew that it was not easy to bring back the party's core voters who had voted twice against it—once in the 2017 municipal elections and then in the 2019 Lok Sabha elections—back to the party fold. A repeat victory in the assembly elections, if not impossible, was definitely going to be an uphill task.

Since all basic premises of measuring the political base of the party had been eroded, the only way forward was to listen up: to listen to the volunteers, to the experts and political observers and, most importantly, to the voters.

༄

2

THE LISTENING POST

Every once in a while comes a film that leaves its mark on the audiences. Long before the likes of Netflix, Amazon Prime or Hotstar started streaming movies into our living rooms, writer, producer and director Rakeysh Omprakash Mehra brought out his labour of love *Rang De Basanti*, a film which he wrote, produced and directed. The year was 2006 and, as films go, it was a risky production. Mehra's previous film *Aks* had failed at the box office and he reportedly spent seven years researching and writing the script for *Rang De Basanti*.

It is also said that films where the lead hero ends up dying usually don't do too well at the box office. In *Rang De Basanti*, all the main protagonists are killed, yet it not only broke all weekend box-office records at the time, but also captured the hearts and minds of moviegoers.

Rang De Basanti is essentially a film about a group of happy-go-lucky friends from Delhi who are asked to act in a British documentary film about India's revolutionary heroes Bhagat Singh, Chandrashekhar Azad, Shivaram Rajguru, Ashfaqulla Khan and Ram Prasad Bismil. At the time of its release, noted film critic Rajeev Masand said that Mehra's film 'accurately captures the spirit and mood of the current generation.'[3]

Jasmine Shah was 25 years old at the time of the film's release. He remembers watching the film and says it changed his life. 'I knew I wanted to do something on policy which would make a positive impact in the lives of people,' says Shah, a mechanical engineer by training and an alumnus of the Indian Institute of Technology (IIT) Madras and Columbia University's School of International and Public Affairs. When he went to watch the film, Shah had a bright career in the corporate sector ahead of him, but the film ignited in him the desire to take a plunge into social work. A few months after watching the film, he started working with the Bengaluru-based not-for-profit organization, Janaagraha.

One of the first big campaigns that Shah worked on was the 'Jaago Re', one billion votes campaign, which was launched in 2008 by Janaagraha in partnership with Tata Tea Limited. The aim of the campaign was to get voters, particularly the youth of India, to sign up and vote in the elections. The 12-member team running the campaign comprised people below the age of 30 and at least five of the 12 members like Shah had given up their corporate jobs to join the campaign.

Interestingly, Rakeysh Omprakash Mehra was one of the members of the advisory board of Janaagraha along with N.R. Narayana Murthy, chairman and chief mentor of Infosys, and T.S. Krishnamurthy, former Chief Election Commissioner of India. Shah says that he and Mehra became good friends and have remained so since then.

---

[3]Rajeev Masand—Movies that matter: From bollywood, hollywood and everywhere else. Available at: http://rajeevmasand.com/admin/category/uncategorized/page/50/, last accessed on 21 July 2020.

When Shah moved to Delhi in 2013, he got in touch with the AAP through his work on policy and education. He started helping the party with its policy on education and governance before joining the Delhi government under the AAP in 2016.

'The AAP is a true start-up,' says Shah, describing his switch from the corporate sector job to an NGO and finally a political party, and adds, 'What the party lacks in expertise, we make up in commitment and enthusiasm.'

Like many in the AAP, Shah has also worn many hats: from being an advisor, to an active manager of volunteers, to finally leading the media campaign for the 2020 elections. He says that the party keeps bouncing back despite some major setbacks because, like a start-up, it has been able to quickly innovate and adapt.

Listen Before You Speak

The mood in 2017 was very different. Continuing its string of losses, the party had failed to form the government in Punjab. The party had been overconfident and had failed to see that not everyone was fully convinced to vote them into power. The party had, in fact, gone to town declaring that it was coming to power in Punjab. Even though people decided to vote out the SAD, which had been in power from 2007 to 2017, voters only gave the AAP 20 seats. Though it could be considered a good performance as the AAP had no presence in the state assembly before that, its tally was nowhere near the numbers needed to form the government.

The humbling experience in Punjab had dampened the spirits in the AAP and that could be seen in the elections to Delhi's three municipal bodies. Here too, the AAP had hoped to replicate its stunning performance of the 2015 Delhi state assembly elections, where it had emerged victorious in 67 of the 70 seats. However, this was not to be: it came a distant second in the municipal elections. The only consolation was that it had replaced the Congress in the second spot in most of the wards.

In Shah's view, the Punjab debacle had resulted in the AAP working with barely 20 per cent enthusiasm for the Delhi municipal elections. The party's performance had, however, not hit rock bottom. Its crushing defeat in the 2019 Lok Sabha elections, where it did not manage to win a single seat in Delhi, was its lowest point. One would expect that the party which had received a clear mandate in the 2015 Delhi state assembly elections and was considered to be the most popular party at the time would do reasonably well, but it not only lost all of the seven seats from Delhi in the 2019 Lok Sabha elections, but was relegated to the third position after the BJP and the Congress. That the party's performance in Delhi had hit rock bottom just eight months before the crucial state assembly polls was a cause for much concern.

The question being asked by everyone, including party insiders, was: how did the AAP misread the mood of the people and that too by such a wide margin? Was this the beginning of the end?

'What we needed to do was to listen to what people had to say about us. What impression did they have of us? Were we not communicating our policies properly? We needed to know and know fast,' says Shah. To do this, the AAP launched a three-layered listening programme. For Shah, who was to be the primary lead for the party's media campaign in the 2020 Delhi elections, this programme was going to be an eye-opener and it was crucial to get the party's messaging right. A three-pronged approach was followed.

Party Leadership's Outreach with Volunteers

With the general mood in the party at an all-time low in the aftermath of the Lok Sabha elections, the party leadership started organizing meetings with its volunteers. Unlike other parties, AAP's primary strength is its core voters, several of whom also volunteer in elections. Both the BJP and the Congress have considerably larger war chests and more financial muscle when it comes to spending on elections. The BJP also banks on the support from Rashtriya Swayamsevak Sangh (RSS) cadres that help in campaigning. The Congress, by its sheer history of being the grand old party of India, has a dedicated structure of party workers, even though it has seen defections, including some high-profile exits over the past couple of years.

A series of 70 meetings with AAP volunteers were held over the course of a couple of months. The purpose was to reassure the volunteers that this was a temporary bump on the road and also to listen to what they may have to say.

While the party did not gather much in terms of inputs to weave a narrative for the assembly elections, these meetings turned out to be very useful in two respects: the volunteers shared what they had heard from voters and it also helped the party reconnect with the volunteers, who felt rejuvenated. The party was able to convince its volunteers that Delhi voters were ready to vote for the AAP in the state and that its volunteers were going to take it to victory.

Socio-economic Groups

The *aam aadmi* or the common man is the biggest voter base of the AAP. It is also the segment which has benefitted the most from various schemes and policies of the government. As part of the 'listening' process, the AAP conducted various surveys among different socio-economic groups to see how the party was being perceived. Based on this feedback, Kejriwal wrote letters to different sections of society which had benefitted from government policies such as the doubling of pension, electricity and water subsidy, and amnesty schemes for defaulters. He also wrote letters to parents of students studying in government schools and those visiting the mohalla clinics.

These letters had a massive impact. They helped build a direct connection between Kejriwal and the people who had benefitted from one scheme or the other launched by the AAP. More importantly, all this was done without any fanfare or noise. It was the first turning point. The people of Delhi started feeling that whatever be their position on issues of national importance, they needed 'Kejriwal in Delhi', that he was someone who cared for them.

It was from here that the AAP picked up its first war cry for the Delhi state assembly elections: '*Dilli men toh Kejriwal!* (In Delhi, it has to be Kejriwal!)'. A slogan devised not by an advertising agency but by party volunteers and workers. It was an instant hit.

These surveys among various socio-economic groups also led to a more scientific and detailed listening on the ground by professionals, before the party went to the drawing board.

Focus Groups

Different focus groups comprising 15 or more people were set up to study how Delhi's voters would react to different scenarios. This exercise was outsourced to independent professionals. Delhi was divided into socio-economic interest groups. People from different age groups, interest groups and economic strata were identified and they participated in group discussions. These were long sessions where the participants discussed different scenarios. Members of the groups were asked several questions ranging from their perception of the AAP, to how they saw the party evolving in the future. Three main points came out of this exercise:

- There was a lot of goodwill about the development work done by the AAP government in Delhi, especially in the area of water supply, electricity, healthcare and education.
- People who had voted for other parties in the Lok Sabha elections were ready to vote for the AAP.
- Kejriwal was Delhi's most popular chief ministerial candidate.

Stop Complaining

All the three exercises conducted to listen were crucial for the party to figure out its weak points and to strategize how it should engage with voters. 'There was also a perception among some of the focus groups that the AAP and Kejriwal complained a lot,' says Shah.

The unique power-sharing in Delhi between the state government, the Centre and the various municipal bodies means that several of the AAP government's schemes would need to be funnelled via the Lt Governor Anil Baijal's office. Some schemes such as the mohalla clinics and the doorstep delivery of services had been pending with the Lt Governor's office for months. While the AAP often complained about this being a deliberate delaying tactic by the Centre, the office of the Lt Governor had maintained that either the Delhi government was overstepping its powers or that the schemes needed a careful study before a formal nod could be given.

Matters really came to a head in February 2018. Anshu

Prakash, who was then the Chief Secretary in the Delhi government, had been summoned by the CM to his house for a meeting at midnight. The AAP had accused Prakash of working at the behest of the BJP and the central government. Prakash had alleged that soon after he arrived for the meeting, an altercation broke out and he was allegedly assaulted by two AAP MLAs who were present there. This, he says, happened in the presence of the CM and other MLAs. One of the MLAs he had named in the complaint countered his words, accusing Prakash of hurling casteist slurs against him and another MLA. Police complaints were also filed by both sides. The incident marked one of the lowest points of the already strained relationship between the AAP government and the Centre.

Following this incident, many government officers decided to adopt a 'go-slow' approach on work allotted to them, as a mark of protest against the Delhi government. This continued for almost four months till Kejriwal, along with his Cabinet ministers, went to meet the Lt Governor at his residence in June 2018. Kejriwal had wanted the Lt Governor to intervene to end the strike by officers and also green-light a proposal to allow door-to-door delivery of food ration to Delhi's citizens. Apparently, since no formal meeting had been scheduled, the Lt Governor did not meet with the CM. Kejriwal and his Cabinet decided to protest by camping out on the sofas in the waiting room of the Lt Governor's office. The party even released some pictures of Kejriwal and his Cabinet colleagues stretched out on pale-carrot-coloured sofas.[4]

---

[4]Swati Chaturvedi, 'Won't Leave This Sofa, This Is a Comfortable Dharna, Says Arvind Kejriwal', NDTV, 13 June 2018. Available at: https://www. ndtv.com/opinion/wont-leave-this-sofa-this-is-a-comfortable-dharna-says-arvind-kejriwal-1866654, last accessed on 21 July 2020.

The photos were quickly used by his critics to ridicule Kejriwal. While some described the move as part of 'Kejriwal's antics', others made light of it, suggesting that the Kejriwal Cabinet was there for the free air conditioning and Wi-Fi, with an obvious reference to AAP's as yet largely unfilled promise of providing free Wi-Fi in Delhi.

In response, Kejriwal released an eight-minute-long video on Twitter. He shot back at his critics saying, 'It isn't easy to sleep on a sofa for four days straight. We are not here to have fun. We're doing this for Delhi's citizens. We could have been sitting in our own homes'. To further make their point, Cabinet members at the sit-in dharna started a hunger strike.

The unprecedented situation continued to make daily headlines. The jokes about Kejriwal also started thinning out on social media as things started getting serious when Deputy CM Manish Sisodia and Health Minister Satyendra Jain, who had been on hunger strike, had to be taken to the hospital because of health complications.

The Indian Administrative Service (IAS) Association of Delhi was forced to call a press conference to clarify its stand. The association said that its officers in Delhi were not on strike but feared being attacked by AAP MLAs, referring to the alleged assault on Prakash.

Soon after the press conference and nine days after it started, the 'sofa dharna' came to an end. Both government officers and Kejriwal's ministers started attending joint meetings. Even though his critics still maintained that the latest stand-off was an engineered crisis, Kejriwal seemed to have won the round, with more people now convinced that the Delhi government was facing hurdles in functioning in Delhi, whatever be the cause.

'The AAP is a start-up and like any start-up, it has to be

a disruptor. We also want to make a mark in delivering for the people and for that we have to break the existing politics-as-usual approach,' says Jasmine Shah, who headed the media campaign for the AAP during the 2020 elections.

The AAP had brought out several schemes, many of which had tangible impact, benefitting not just the poor but even the middle and upper classes. However, the image in the minds of the people was that the AAP either complained a lot or just made announcements. This, according to Shah, needed to change.

While Kejriwal's complaining may have won him some sympathy, voters still expected him to get the job done. 'No one likes a constantly nagging child and that image of the government needed to be changed,' explains Shah. There was also a realization within the AAP that no matter how much complaining Kejriwal did, the various power structures in Delhi were not changing anytime soon, and the only way forward was to accept this reality and yet try and meet the aspirations of voters.

'Even with the limitations we were facing, we wanted to show the voters of Delhi that they were getting the biggest and best bang for their buck,' says Shah, who is credited with developing Delhi's first comprehensive Outcome Budget for 2017–18. The idea was to bring in greater transparency and efficiency in governance, and link the money being spent to actual delivery of goods and services.

Shah, who graduated in 2012 with a Master of Public Administration from Columbia University's School of International and Public Affairs, had also worked with 10 different governments while he was with the Massachusetts Institute of Technology's Jameel Poverty Action Lab (J-PAL) at the International Growth Centre. These skills would prove invaluable in getting the different governments and departments to talk to each other and get projects off the ground in Delhi.

Recap and Rejuvenation

Getting projects off the ground wasn't the only problem. Voters were unsure of how committed the AAP was to Delhi. The fact that the party's focus lately had been the Punjab elections and the charge by the Opposition that Kejriwal was gunning to be the CM of Punjab had not gone down too well with the party and its volunteers. What was needed was damage control to lift the morale within the party and shore up its image in Delhi.

To start with, Kejriwal sat down for TV interviews with several channels. The focus was clear. The defender Kejriwal had challenged the opponents to contest the election on the work done by his government. Kejriwal showcased the transformation in sectors such as healthcare and education. He made it a point to say that for the first time a government had delivered more than it had promised. As Shah says, 'It was for the first time that a party in power was contesting elections based solely on the work it had done.' With this strategic move, if any opponent wanted to take a swipe at the AAP, they had to discuss the projects carried out by the Delhi government.

Kejriwal also did not miss the opportunity to contrast the work done by his government with what he saw as mis-governance by the three municipal bodies in Delhi. If the BJP tried to make this a much larger election by trying to corner the AAP over issues such as the attack on students in Jawaharlal Nehru University (JNU) or the Citizenship (Amendment) Act (CAA), 2019, Kejriwal would ask the spokespersons from the

BJP to show a comparative school in the three municipal bodies under the BJP in Delhi or any of the states under the BJP or the Congress. By doing so, Kejriwal ensured that he was setting the narrative.

Next was the issue of the CM. While Kejriwal was the AAP's projected CM candidate for the 2020 Delhi assembly elections, the BJP and the Congress had not announced any CM candidate. The AAP exploited this to its advantage. 'How serious were the other two if they cannot even decide who their CM candidate will be?' Kejriwal would often challenge his opponents in his political rallies and speeches.

In addition to the one-on-one discussions and debates on television, another strategy was to get Kejriwal to hold more regular press conferences. The aim was to keep the focus on development and how the AAP planned to deliver on various fronts. The narrative needed to shift from the loss in the Lok Sabha polls to how the party was changing Delhi with its good governance.

The AAP had already successfully highlighted that the BJP had Modi, but it didn't have a CM candidate for Delhi. Closer to the elections, the AAP adopted another tact. While earlier press conferences had been jointly held, usually along with Cabinet ministers, the AAP now started fielding Kejriwal alone—no co-chair, no other Cabinet colleague, just Kejriwal. The idea was to put the focus on Kejriwal and show that there was no other candidate for the top job.

Dropping Sitting MLAs

The listening surveys also threw up another problem. While voters seemed convinced about Kejriwal's candidature, they were unhappy with several of their local MLAs. As a result, the AAP decided to drop 15 sitting MLAs in the 2020 Delhi elections. The strategy worked, and the AAP managed to win 14 of the 15 seats where the sitting MLAs had been replaced with alternative candidates.

The BJP had adopted the same strategy with huge success in the 2017 Delhi municipal elections. Keen to shed the unresponsive, inefficient and corrupt tag about corporators from the three municipalities, the BJP decided to not field even a single sitting counsellor. Instead, new faces were drafted in and given tickets. The gambit worked; the BJP comfortably managed to win all three corporations, with the AAP coming a distant second.

Getting the Messaging Right

At the heart of the AAP is the *aam aadmi*, the common man. Everything that the party does–its government schemes and policies, selection of candidates to even the way its ministers and CM dress—largely underscores that.

But how do you convince voters that ordinary men and women can do extraordinary things, especially in politics? To make matters worse for the AAP, the string of losses in elections further added to the feeling that the voters had perhaps lost confidence in the party. It was tough to avoid the obvious question: should politics be left to professional politicians after all? The BJP even called Kejriwal an 'Urban Naxal' and accused the party of not knowing how to govern. The AAP had to change that image and do it fast.

It was in mid-2019 that Jasmine Shah was asked by the AAP to head its media campaign and help cultivate the right image for the party.

'I see myself more as a policy person rather than a

politician,' Shah tells us. 'I had worked in the Delhi government before the elections and so I knew what we were doing for the city; the trick was how to communicate this to the people.'

Shah himself admits that the messaging for the 2017 municipal polls was not clear. He says, 'We didn't really have much to show then of what we had done, merely making proclamations was not going to help either.'

The AAP decided to prepare a 30-point report card highlighting the work it had done and how things were already helping make an impact in people's lives. This yellow-coloured report card looked exactly like the student report cards issued by schools. It talked about the achievements of the government in 10 key areas such as transformation in education and healthcare sectors, cheap and uninterrupted power supply, free water supply, highest minimum wages, per capita income and surplus revenue of the government, women's safety and free bus rides for women, work in unauthorized colonies, public transport, doorstep delivery of services, free pilgrimage scheme for senior citizens, free Wi-Fi and the government's ratings. The idea was to tell the people of Delhi that their government was accountable and was ready to put forward its performance for public scrutiny.

Next, the party challenged the Opposition to nominate anyone as its chief ministerial candidate to face Kejriwal in a debate. While the AAP was ready for the debate, the challenge also underscored the fact that neither the BJP nor the Congress had announced a chief ministerial candidate. Kejriwal was by default the only chief ministerial candidate in the race and that was the message that the AAP wanted to send to the voters.

Next, the party deployed a team of researchers whose only job was to get the latest data on government schemes and a reality check about various projects on the ground. While the

AAP had earlier boycotted some TV channels which, according to it, were biased against the party, it now changed its position and started sending its spokespersons for the evening TV debates even on those channels.

'We realized that even when we were not sending a spokesperson to a particular channel's TV debate, the channel would get someone who had either claimed to have worked with the AAP or had been a supporter of the party. This way, the TV channel got a good shouting match, [and] the AAP was losing ground despite not being present in the debates to explain its position,' says Shah.

The AAP also started sending out a list of its official spokespersons to all news outlets. The message was clear: it was only 'official' if it came from an official party spokesperson, not someone a TV channel had found to fill the studio guest chair. 'We had put in a lot of systems in place to make sure that our spokespersons were speaking in one voice and [on] how to bring back the discussion to development,' says Shah. The AAP had started a daily briefing for its spokespersons, and the research team would provide detailed summaries of all the main programmes of the party and what issues had been raised by the Opposition that day. The results were beginning to show.

Countering Hindutva with Hanuman Chalisa

As the campaign neared its end, the BJP also stepped up its personal attacks against Kejriwal—from calling him a terrorist to being anti-Hindu. Interestingly, Kejriwal, when asked by the anchor of a live TV show whether he was a 'Hanuman *bhakt*' (a follower of the Hindu god Hanuman), responded, 'I am not only an ardent follower but also a regular at the

Hanuman temple'. Next, when asked whether he could recite the Hanuman Chalisa (the holy book of verses addressed to Hanuman), Kejriwal gladly complied to the cheering of the studio audience. Over the next few days, Kejriwal was asked the same question by other TV anchors and each time, he happily sang the hymn.

The BJP candidate from Delhi's Model Town seat created further controversy when he tweeted that 'Kejriwal has started reading the Hanuman Chalisa and now [Asaduddin] Owaisi [All India Majlis-E-Ittehadul Muslimeen (AIMIM) leader and Hyderabad MP] will also start reading it'. Kapil Mishra, a former AAP minister, had been a bitter critic of Kejriwal after he was sacked from the Cabinet in May 2017. While he had denied having any plans at the time of his sacking, Mishra eventually joined the BJP and was fielded in the 2020 Delhi elections.

Jasmine Shah sums up the entire episode for us: 'The fact that Kejriwal knew the Hanuman Chalisa by heart and was willing to recite it, not only countered the BJP's claim that he was anti-Hindu, but also ensured that the BJP's boast that Kejriwal was forced to do so, did not go down well with Delhi's voters, who felt that the BJP was behaving like a bully. The underdog does have his day.'

ᔆᔆ

3

THE DELHI SEQUEL

During the last two elections in 2013 and 2015, Kejriwal himself had been the chief strategist of the party, with his core team of mostly lesser-known backroom boys handling different departments and reporting directly to him. From outdoor advertising and content generation to outreach and media management, Kejriwal would micromanage everything. It had, no doubt, been tricky, as there was nothing—from fundraisers to strategy sessions to public meetings—that he could afford to skip. It turned him into a 24x7 machine. He would wake up at around 3.30 a.m., read his emails and messages, and start calling his team members 6 a.m. onwards. The core group of managers would meet at his flat in Kaushambi in Ghaziabad at 8 a.m. Back-to-back meetings with different teams would follow. The various teams would update him on surveys conducted on the party's vote share, standing of probable candidates in constituencies, selection of candidates, positive and negative coverage in the media and media plans for the week.

A typical day for Kejriwal would end late in the night. But that was only for 'manager Kejriwal'. 'Leader Kejriwal' had an even more hectic life. His tight roadshow and public-meeting schedules often ended up with him skipping meals, which can be dangerous for a diabetic like him. In the middle of all this, he would also have media interactions lined up. In the run-up to the elections, Kejriwal had started to lose weight. He was looking pale, tired and completely exhausted. But then, you can't look tired and exhausted on TV screens, and in rallies and roadshows. After all, leaders have to be more than 'mere mortals', or at least appear to be so.

The same routine was on the cards for this sequel of his home production too. Kejriwal had to wear two hats: he was both the hero and the director of the film. The listening part of the exercise had been done. The team was working on feedback that had come from on-ground interactions with volunteers, as well as inputs from sympathizers and experts. This time, the party had also hired professionals to conduct focus group discussions to understand the needs, expectations and aspirations of different classes of voters. It was time to go to the drawing board with the wisdom drawn from these feedbacks.

Two things that had emerged quite clearly from all those initiatives were that Kejriwal had a distinct edge over the others as there was a lot of positivity about the work done by the AAP government in Delhi and that he was far more popular than any of his challengers. The BJP and the Congress had missed the importance of projecting chief ministerial nominees, and their campaigns had no face at the forefront. The entire campaign of the AAP was to be woven around this distinguishing factor.

The New Avatar of Kejriwal

The two past elections had also revolved around Kejriwal. First, it was Kejriwal the revolutionary. The party had emerged out of an agitation and Delhi had been its epicentre. Somehow, the people of Delhi had a firm belief that 'these youngsters can bring about change'. Social activist Anna Hazare and his associates had fought very well, but the agitation had failed to extract the Jan Lokpal Bill from the government of the day. People wanted a victory for the movement, and the fact that the AAP grew from the movement culminated in the party's stunning electoral performance under the leadership of Kejriwal.

The dream, however, was short-lived, as Kejriwal had to resign just 49 days later. The people of Delhi were left hugely disappointed. The BJP misread the disappointment as a wave of anger against Kejriwal. While there was some amount of anger among the public, who felt that Kejriwal should have at least tried to run the government instead of 'running away', his public apology did help to do some damage control. The people of Delhi seemed willing to give the tax officer-turned-politician another chance.

The second election centred around 'Paanch Saal Kejriwal', a request to give Kejriwal and the AAP a full five-year term to perform and deliver on promises that they had made. One of the things that worked in favour of the AAP was the image of corrupt officials being arrested and put behind bars during Kejriwal's rather short first stint of 49 days as the CM of Delhi. Another positive memory that the public associated with AAP's first stint was of the electricity tariffs being slashed to half, which was nothing less than a miracle to them. The voters decided to give the AAP a second chance and how! The party emerged with a robust majority, winning 67 of the 70 seats in Delhi.

As they say, no two elections are the same. This third election was entirely different from the earlier two, and Kejriwal knew this only too well. With all the feedback coming from various directions, the biggest question was: what should be upheld as Kejriwal's new avatar? What would sync with the people's current expectations from him?

After several meetings and brainstorming sessions, the party leadership unanimously agreed on projecting 'Kejriwal, the Governance Superman' as the new avatar. The entire campaign was to revolve around this new avatar. The idea was coined on 22 July 2019 and it was finalized within a week.

The Contrast

An ordinary-looking man in his trademark half-sleeved shirt, with an inexpensive Reynolds pen tucked into his shirt pocket and basic chappals for footwear, Kejriwal's public image was that of a common man. It was hard to believe that the same Kejriwal could lead a team of ministers and bureaucrats that had performed a complete turnaround in the fields of healthcare, education, water and electricity supply, and various other areas in just five years. But the fact was that he had done so successfully. The idea was to marry Kejriwal's image as a common man with that of a CM who had proved to be a 'Governance Superman'.

It was not too difficult to merge the two images and make people believe that this ordinary-looking person had indeed pulled off this miracle of good governance. Several generations have, after all, been raised on tales of superheroes leading two different lives. Fictional characters such as Peter Parker, who leads the life of a common man and doubles up as the superhero Spiderman, and Clarke Kent as Superman were discussed in the meetings.

A similar narrative had to be built for Kejriwal. Stories were to be woven around how Kejriwal had cracked the IIT exams and held an engineering degree from one of India's most prestigious engineering colleges; how he worked with Mother Teresa's Missionaries of Charity; how he had left a promising career as a civil servant to become an activist, an agent of change and an awardee of the prestigious Ramon Magsaysay Award in 2006. There were indeed several threads that could contribute to this narrative.

To connect the two images, it was decided to project how Kejriwal had led this team of world-class professionals and experts who had conceived and implemented pro-people schemes, such as mohalla clinics and doorstep delivery of services, which had won appreciation from across the globe. Strategically, contrasts were to be made with other governments, showing how no other CM could match or deliver what Kejriwal had delivered in five years, from 2015 to 2020.

Mass Contact Programme

It was Kejriwal's idea to write to every single beneficiary of the Delhi government's flagship schemes, even though the number of beneficiaries ran into millions. These included people who had benefitted from subsidies on electricity and water bills, those drawing old-age and widow pensions, parents of those studying in government schools and individuals benefitting from mohalla clinics. Essentially, almost every person who had benefitted from government schemes was contacted.

This had a massive feel-good factor and helped to build a bond with the citizens. A personal letter from the CM was not merely an exercise to remind the public of the benefits they had reaped, but also to establish a personal rapport with them.

The letters were carefully crafted to give the recipients

the feel of a family member writing to them. Like many of his communications, Kejriwal drafted this letter as well. Written as a personal letter to a friend or family member, the idea was that the recipient would keep this as a personal keepsake, a reminder of a link between themselves and Kejriwal.

Major subsidy-driven schemes had been launched at the beginning of his government's tenure, including free units of water and subsidized electricity. Five years is a long time. Though people still acknowledged that the benefits were indeed given to them by the Kejriwal government, a feeling of entitlement had also crept in. These letters were very helpful in renewing the relationship based on a sense that yes, this government had brought people personal and visible benefits.

Family Touch

One of the aims of this mass contact programme was also to establish and portray Kejriwal as 'the elder son of the family'. As a communication strategy, the statements of the key party spokespersons and Kejriwal himself were so designed that they conveyed this relationship with the voter. Every time his team members spoke to the media or the public, they made sure that they called Kejriwal 'the elder son of every family in Delhi'.

In later speeches, media interactions and town halls, Kejriwal elaborated on this. 'I consider myself as "*bada beta* (elder son)" of every family in Delhi, whose responsibility is to pay the electricity bill, water bill, take patients to clinics for treatment and arrange pilgrimages for the elders of the family. And I am doing so and shall continue doing so, in future as well,' he reiterated in almost every public address. This approach resulted in building a rapport with the people, which was to reap dividends later.

As the elections drew close, the attacks on Kejriwal grew more personal and scathing. BJP leader and MP Parvesh Verma went on to call Kejriwal 'a terrorist'[5]. As if that was not enough, Union Minister and in-charge of Delhi elections for the BJP, Prakash Javadekar also repeated the statement.[6] This gave the AAP an opportunity to retaliate with their point of view, and the party spokesperson went on every channel, repeating what the BJP had called Kejriwal. They asked other panellists and audiences whether the BJP was referring to the son of every household of Delhi as a terrorist. Counterquestions were posed by AAP spokespersons: do terrorists take elders on pilgrimages? Do terrorists build world-class schools for children? Do terrorists open mohalla clinics? The people of Delhi will give a befitting reply to the BJP, the spokespersons declared.

This response created huge sympathy for Kejriwal. Even fence sitters, who had been unsure about which way they would be voting, thought that the BJP had gone too far in calling Kejriwal a 'terrorist'. They felt that while Kejriwal could be called several other things, calling him a terrorist just did not fit the man they knew—that single statement backfired on the BJP.

---

[5]Outlook Web Bureau, 'EC Bans BJP's Parvesh Verma From Campaigning For Calling Delhi CM Kejriwal "Terrorist", *Outlook*, 5 February 2020. Available at: https://www.outlookindia.com/website/story/india-news-election-commission-bans-parvesh-verma-from-campaigning-for-calling-delhi-cm-kejriwal-terrorist/346834, last accessed on 24 July 2020.
[6]ANI, 'Arvind Kejriwal a Terrorist, Plenty of Proofs Available: Prakash Javadekar', *The Economic Times*, 4 February 2020. Available at: https://economictimes.indiatimes.com/news/politics-and-nation/arvind-kejriwal-is-a-terrorist-theres-plenty-of-proof-says-prakash-javadekar/videoshow/73910422.cms, last accessed on 24 July 2020.

Kejriwal's Suraksha Chakra

The listening exercise had revealed that brand Kejriwal enjoyed huge credibility among the voters of Delhi. They believed that Kejriwal delivered on his promises. This aspect of the brand led the team to come up with the idea of a thrust to 'Kejriwal's Suraksha Chakra'. The idea was first suggested in the first week of September 2019. The party did not have any big-ticket promises to make in the manifesto. At one point, it was considering presenting 'Kejriwal's Suraksha Chakra' as the main election promise. The idea was to give all Delhiites 'Kejriwal's guarantee of free and quality education and healthcare'. This was Kejriwal's most ambitious project, which would undoubtedly take a few years to be fully implemented. He had almost made up his mind to announce this in the second week of September, but for some reason, the announcement had to be pushed back and was revived later on 19 January 2020 in a new avatar.

BJP's propaganda machinery had launched a massive whisper campaign in the city, claiming that all subsidy-driven schemes would be withdrawn after 31 March 2020 by the AAP government. To counter this, on 19 January, Kejriwal launched his 'Guarantee Card', which guaranteed 10 things:

1. 24×7 uninterrupted power supply; 200 units of free electricity scheme to continue for the next five years; overground cables to be removed and electricity to be supplied only through underground cables
2. 24×7 water supply; 20,000 litres of free water scheme to continue for the next five years
3. World-class education up to graduation shall be ensured for every Delhiite

4. World-class healthcare facilities would be provided through modern hospitals and mohalla clinics
5. More than 11,000 new buses would be added to the fleet and 500 km of new Metro line were to be laid
6. A three-time decrease in pollution level, a promise to plant more than two crore trees and clean the Yamuna
7. A garbage-free Delhi
8. CCTV cameras, street lights, bus marshals and mohalla marshals to be provided for the safety of women
9. All unauthorized colonies to be provided roads, drinking water, sewage disposal, mohalla clinics and CCTV cameras
10. '*Jahan jhuggi, wahaan makaan* (Shanties to be replaced by pucca houses)'

This guarantee card was a major strategic point. In effect, the AAP was offering to make the lives of lakhs of people much more liveable, for the first time. The promise of water, electricity, education, healthcare and safety for women was such that it forced the voter to stop and give a lot more weightage to the potential being offered by Kejriwal.

Finger on the Pulse

No strategy can be static. Election campaigns are constantly moving and evolving. An effective communication war also works the same way and there is always a need to tweak a little. Fine-tuning campaigns, especially communication, is possible only if you have your finger on the pulse of your voters. For the last three elections in Delhi, Kejriwal has used his army of ground volunteers effectively for two purposes: for extensive door-to-door campaigning and for collecting dynamic feedback from voters.

The door-to-door exercises are planned, executed and monitored centrally by the party. But the volunteers don't just go to canvass votes for the party. Most often, they go with a questionnaire in hand. The questions are drafted to get the voter to think. In their effort to seek answers from within, the voter encounters facts they are already aware of but which may not have been central to their process of deciding who they would vote for.

These questionnaires have proved very helpful in converting fence sitters. Very quickly, they were able to move away from the propaganda statements of the Opposition and see their benefit in voting for the AAP. There were three major door-to-door exercises carried out before the 2020 assembly elections. This included a door-to-door survey to find out the mood of voters as well as a 'Lage Raho Kejriwal (Keep at it Kejriwal)' pamphlet campaign which endorsed Kejriwal as AAP's CM nominee for the 2020 elections. The last one was to deliver the guarantee card, in the shape of a table calendar. Kejriwal would personally take feedback from the soldiers on the ground and then fine-tune the strategy accordingly.

In each of the campaigns, Kejriwal had been instrumental in giving it shape or fine-tuning the strategies for maximum impact. Both as 'leader' and 'manager', Kejriwal had done a fine balancing act. He would need it for the biggest political fight of his life soon.

ᄋᄀ

4

CALM, LOGICAL PEOPLE

'We are a calm, logical people now,' AAP National Executive member, Preeti Sharma Menon says with a straight face. It is tough to make out whether Menon, sitting in her flat in Mumbai, is being serious or sarcastic. The only option is to let the moment linger, hoping that her poker face will provide the slightest of clues. Instead, the next 10 seconds seem to stretch for perhaps a full minute. She gives nothing away, and it is we who choose to break the silence.

'Arvind Kejriwal and his Cabinet were doing a dharna on the Delhi Lt Governor's sofa for close to nine days!' we remind her and add, 'Remember, much before that, the Delhi CM had made headlines nationwide when he slept on the pavement near Parliament House, in the dead of winter, demanding action against some police officers? The Opposition has described Kejriwal and the AAP as anarchists. So, won't these actions by Kejriwal seem to only reinforce what the Opposition is saying?'

'Ah! But each time we did this, there was a reason and logic behind it. More so now,' Menon says, this time with a big smile. As the party spokesperson and in-charge of volunteers, she is also one of its most outspoken leaders and active personalities in the AAP.

Menon's own life perhaps in some way mirrors the ups and downs of the AAP. Both have had their fair share of successes and failures, desertions and accomplishments. As one of the founding members of the party and an executive member, perhaps no one understands the pulse of the party and its volunteer base better than her.

'You see, the expectations from the AAP are immense. We are a political disruptor. We keep saying that we are not here for the power and it's our ideology for clean and effective governance which drives us, but at the same time, if we don't win, then it will be said that it is our ideology that has failed,' says Menon.

'All the dharnas, street-side protests, even by the sitting CM, were necessary to carve out a space for the new kid on the block,' she says, referring to the AAP. 'Other parties have their entrenched thoughts and stated views. Even without them commenting on some of the issues, most people already know where they stand. We had to build a momentum to tell people what we stand for,' she explains.

As she sits calmly, it becomes apparent why Menon is one of AAP's main troubleshooters and chief organizers, both roles requiring not only a lot of endurance but also sharp strategies. However, as Menon says, till some years ago, 'politics' was the last thing on her mind.

Menon says that just being efficient at her job and life had been her main drivers. It was August 2011 and Anna Hazare's India Against Corruption (IAC) protest had been creating a storm in not just the national capital but across the country. The United Progressive Alliance (UPA)-led government at the Centre had miscalculated the growing resentment against corruption and the impression of there being a policy paralysis in the central government. Then, the government took a series of political missteps, including the arrest of Hazare, who was sent to Delhi's Tihar jail. This only made matters worse for the central government and ignited a nationwide protest with hundreds of thousands lending their voices to support Hazare's main demand. They wanted Parliament to enact a law to set up a 'Lokpal', an ombudsman to oversee the review of all cases of corruption from the lowest official to the highest, including the Prime Minister's Office (PMO).

To build pressure, Hazare, upon his release from jail, went on a hunger strike at Ramlila Maidan in the capital. On 21 August, the seventh day of this fast, the IAC campaigners asked for a show of support. While over a hundred thousand people turned up in support of Hazare's demand at Ramlila Maidan, there were also massive supportive rallies across the country, including in Mumbai, where around 50,000 people took part in a rally demanding the release of Hazare and to enact the anti-corruption law. By Mumbai standards, this is quite an impressive number.

Popular music composer Vishal Dadlani was one of those who had been closely following what was happening in Delhi and had been to Ramlila Maidan in the capital where Hazare had been holding his protest. 'Dadlani called me and told me that I had to go to Delhi and to Ramlila Maidan. I told him that he had gone mad and there was no way I was getting involved in anything like this,' says Menon.

Dadlani persisted and so, a few days later, when IAC called for nationwide protests, Menon went to the one organized in Mumbai. According to her, 'I went there as a tourist and came back a fully converted campaigner.'

Menon, who just three years earlier had sold her hugely successful training company for ₹40 crore, had been wanting to do something more meaningful with her life. She had started Viira Cabs, a Mumbai-based taxi company with exclusively women drivers. She saw this as a means to provide employment to women, and at the same time, empower them. Unfortunately, it was not the huge success she had been hoping for. 'We trained over 200 women drivers, but our cab fleet never went beyond 25 cars,' she admits. In fact, most of her women trainee drivers had never even set foot inside a car. Compared to most of them, men not only were more familiar with cars, many of them already had driving licences.

'When I went to the IAC protest site that day in Mumbai, I realized that this was how I was going to bring about a change in India,' says Menon. The cab company owner was so excited that she soon put her cab company and its drivers to work for the campaign. 'Initially, there had been no office space for IAC in Mumbai, and very often, campaign materials had to be stored somewhere. I offered our cabs and very often, the campaign materials, including pamphlets, posters and banners, would be kept in the boots of the cabs overnight as temporary storage spaces, to be delivered where the protest was happening next,' shares Menon.

Menon says that her professional strength in operations came in handy when helping with the IAC campaign. 'I realized that organizing and detailing were what the campaign needed the most in Mumbai.' Menon says that after helping to sort out logistics, she also took active part in fundraising, media coordination, organization and managing merchandise. The trainer-turned-businesswoman was increasingly spending more and more time with IAC and after the split in the group in 2012, from which Kejriwal and others decided to form the AAP, Menon was appointed the Secretary of the party's Maharashtra wing. Unable to devote any time to the cab company, Viira Cabs was shut down by Menon in 2014. Menon had by that time been tasked with leading the charge for the AAP in the Lok Sabha elections in Maharashtra.

With the AAP only managing to win four seats, all from Punjab, Menon resigned as state secretary, though she continued to be a member of the AAP.

For Menon, both Viira Cabs and the AAP had been formed with the idea of bringing about change and progress in the country. However, both had run into rough weather. With the two experiences, it seemed that both the business maverick and the political anarchist had to go through a further learning curve.

Romance Can Only Take You Some Distance

The 2015 Delhi assembly elections had been won on romanticism. The AAP had formed a government in 2013 with the support of the Congress, a party it had sworn to vanquish after coming to power. The government lasted for 49 days before Kejriwal declared that the Congress was being unsupportive and resigned. The BJP accused the AAP of being a 'bhagoda' or coward who could not run the government. Yet, despite the odds, the AAP returned to power with a historic landslide victory, winning 67 of the 70 seats in the 2015 Delhi assembly elections. This happened even though the AAP had little to show in terms of its accomplishments in the past. It had made many promises during the 2013 elections but had not been able to deliver on most, as its government then had lasted only for 49 days. That voters still chose to repose their faith in the party in the 2015 assembly elections and the party's dazzling victory can only be described as romanticism and a belief held by many in the nation's capital that since the existing political system had proved to be bereft of anything worthwhile to offer the citizens of the country, perhaps an alternative system in politics, led by mavericks, was the last remaining hope.

AAP's landslide victory in 2015 was indicative of the fact that even despite cynicism about politics, people were willing to hold out hope for a better alternative. But there is only so much that can ride on just romance. Psychologists say that in romantic relationships, people are generally either realists or romantics: very rarely are they both.

So, if the AAP had won the 2015 elections on romanticism, it was equally important for the party to prove itself in the next five years, when voters would demand more realism and were less likely to be swayed by just romance a second time.

And it was not just the voters. 'We as a party and ideology are where the Left parties started. We are a cadre-based party and unlike the Congress or the BJP, where people join a party which has existing long-established structures and even paid staff positions, the AAP is held together by the idealism and hopes of many in the community,' says Menon.

As the person in charge of volunteers, Menon says that their role cannot be emphasized enough. She says, 'Almost all the people who have joined our party have done so because they want to bring about a change in politics. There must be the romance of belief, but we needed to ensure both for our voters as well as for our volunteers, that we deliver on the promises we had made.'

In fact, one of the big differences between the 2015 and 2020 election campaigns was the role of the volunteers and how they were guided. As Menon shares, 'In 2015, our volunteers used to often bring their own food and even small donations to help fund elections. This time around, we were a little more organized and were able deploy them where they could be the most useful.'

Menon says that while the AAP does not have the kind of budget that big parties such as the BJP or the Congress have, the party tries to ensure that it always remains receptive to its volunteers and what they were saying. 'When you have people who are emotionally charged and have strong beliefs, you have to be even more cautious about their emotions and feelings and how you deal with them,' she says.

For the 2020 campaign, the AAP had launched the 'Kejriwal Phir Se' campaign and asked citizens to express their desire to see Kejriwal re-elected as the CM of Delhi by giving a missed call on a mobile number. The launch coincided with the seventh foundation day of the party on 26 November 2019. 'Over 1.38 lakh people called the number to connect with Kejriwal and the party. These were all people who wanted to get attached to the party. They all had ideas on what the party should do and how they wanted to contribute. It was important that we reach out to them and utilize their strengths,' says Menon.

While the AAP contacted all the volunteers who had called in to connect with the party, 30,000 of them were actually roped in for various tasks and responsibilities for the Delhi poll campaign.

With volunteers coming in from several states, the AAP deployed them in areas where people of those regions and communities were in greater numbers. 'While the message to voters was the same, it has greater acceptance if it's coming from a person of the same region,' says Menon.

Menon says that the BJP had deployed this same strategy in the 2020 elections, which did give it a boost in getting the message across. According to her, BJP volunteers from Sonipat in Haryana were specifically brought in to campaign in the Pitampura area of Delhi, where many from Sonipat have settled over the years. A similar exercise was undertaken in other parts of Delhi. Volunteers from other states were deployed in those parts of Delhi where people from the same region had settled.

AAP volunteers, particularly those from outside Delhi, worked with different candidates and were given responsibilities. Very often, the party offices of candidates or/ and existing MLAs were used as places for volunteers to stay at night. To keep costs down, if volunteers had to travel, they were encouraged to use the Delhi Metro; only if needed, an Ola or Uber cab was allowed. Travel money could be reimbursed, but for that, receipts or screen grabs of bills had to be provided.

Menon herself moved to Delhi a couple of months before the election and ended up staying in the guest room of the Delhi assembly speaker and party MP Bhagwant Mann. 'The party did not have funds to hire hotels or guest houses and this is how we tried to save money for the campaign,' shares Menon.

'The biggest task in managing volunteers is to ensure that they feel respected and believe that their views are being heard,' says Menon. As in-charge of volunteer management, particularly of those from other states, she says that it is one of the toughest jobs and it is not always possible to ensure that issues don't crop up.

Aaya Ram Gaya Ram

Leaders often switch sides ahead of elections and the AAP has had its share of comings and goings. Ashoka University's Trivedi Centre for Political Data (TCPD) conducted a survey which showed that only eight out of the 37 candidates who switched sides were able to win—just a little over 20 per cent. Interestingly, of the eight who benefitted from jumping ship and changing parties, seven had joined the AAP ahead of the

Delhi polls and managed to cross the finish line.

Out of the eight contestants who quit the AAP, only Anil Kumar Bajpai, who had won from the Gandhi Nagar seat in 2015 on an AAP ticket, managed to retain his seat. Kapil Mishra, who had been a minster in the AAP government and had been suspended before joining the BJP in 2019, lost his Model Town seat to the AAP candidate.

Another prominent candidate, former Chandni Chowk MLA Alka Lamba, who had quit the AAP to rejoin the Congress party ahead of the polls, lost her seat. Interestingly, Lamba, a student union leader from Delhi, who started her political career with the Congress, joined the AAP before the 2015 polls and then switched back to the Congress in 2019.

Menon defends the inclusion of candidates from other parties into the AAP and their fielding ahead of the polls. 'It's obvious that other parties have been around a lot longer than the AAP. If other party politicians can see that we are doing something right, why shall we not allow them as long as they believe in our ideology?' asks Menon.

Ideology or not, the fact is that the AAP has certainly matured both in the way it has handled the exit of leaders from the party and also in gauging the winnability of candidates joining the party.

∽

5

THE GAME CHANGER

'The BJP did a surgical strike in Balakot when it struck terror camps in Pakistan, [and] I thought what we needed was a surgical strike of our own,' Satyendra Jain tells us. Dressed in light-blue jeans and an untucked white-and-blue cotton check shirt, there is a certain casual and relaxed air about him.

We are on the seventh-floor office of Satyendra Jain, architect-turned-politician and one of Kejriwal's most trusted aides and versatile Cabinet ministers. The sixth to ninth floors of the Delhi Secretariat building, situated on the banks of the Yamuna River, are reserved for the Cabinet ministers of the Delhi government and top key officials. It also provides an enviable vista of the city below.

Just beyond the tall eucalyptus trees lining the road that goes past the secretariat building, one can see the Yamuna as it slowly makes its way through Delhi before heading towards Agra and eventually merging with the Ganges at Prayagraj (formerly Allahabad). The spotlessly clean double-glazed glass windows proudly do their job of providing Delhi's top administrators a bird's-eye view of the city while keeping at bay the constant humdrum of the streets below. A little further on, cars and buses continuously fight for space on the busy

Yamuna bridge, their frantic jostling perhaps matched by the steady stream of officers regularly coming with files for Jain to review. Jain waves them towards his desk, where the growing stack of files is beginning to resemble the towering skyscrapers across the Yamuna.

'Apart from radically improving government schools and hospitals, we have been providing Delhiites with 20,000 free units of water every month, electricity at half rates, and recently, free travel for women on board the city's buses and Metro system,' says Jain.

Critics of the schemes, including the BJP and the Congress, have accused the AAP of trying to win the election by giving out 'freebies'. They also argue that by providing 20,000 units of water free every month, it has encouraged wastage of water, something the city can ill afford to do. Jain, however, is quick to defend this.

'India is a socialist republic. That means that it is the responsibility of the state to take care of its citizens. Providing affordable and effective healthcare and education along with essentials such as water and electricity are after all the state's responsibility,' he says. 'The poor don't have washing machines or gardens where they would need more water.'

Jain points towards a full-page newspaper cutting tacked to a board running along one side of his desk. 'Have you ever seen such a government clinic?' the headline reads in Hindi. Below the caption are several coloured pictures of AAP's flagship mohalla clinic or neighbourhood/community clinics. While the colour of the pictures have paled with time, Jain's eyes light up as he talks to us about AAP's initial flagship welfare schemes.

'We had initially announced that we were going to build a thousand such mohalla clinics, but the going was not easy, as we faced resistance from the local municipal corporations and from the Centre,' Jain shares with us.

Delhi's unique structure both as a city state as well as India's capital has resulted in the evolution of several distinct power and administrative centres. The city government, including the ministers and CM, are elected from among 70 assembly constituent seats in the capital. While the city government calls the shots on education, health, electricity, water and public works, there are also three municipal corporations which are responsible for a host of services, some of them with overlapping roles, including municipal schools. The municipal corporations are responsible for a wide range of things, from the registration of births and deaths, to approving building permissions, to collecting and disposing of Delhi's mountains of trash.

Then there is the VVIP section of the capital, comprising the central district which houses the Parliament, the President's sprawling estate, embassies and numerous central government ministries, all of which fall under the jurisdiction of the New Delhi Municipal Council (NDMC). Maintaining law and order is the responsibility of the central government, with more than 85,000 men, women and officers of the Delhi Police reporting to the Home Ministry. To make matters even more complicated, a large chunk of land in Delhi is owned and controlled by the Delhi Development Authority (DDA), which reports to the Centre.

In 2014, Kejriwal, quoting US Senator the late Edward Kennedy, had announced: 'Healthcare is a right and not a privilege.' He promised that his government would open over a thousand mohalla clinics by 2020, which would also mark the end of his second term as CM. All the clinics were to be free and provide free health check-ups, consultations and medicines, in a bid to make basic healthcare accessible to all.

Despite the ambitious target, work on the mohalla clinics began only in 2017, when the Lt Governor of Delhi gave the go-ahead. Jain blames the delay on the ongoing tussle between the Delhi government and the Centre. According to him, even after getting the green signal from the Lt Governor's office, there was a tug of war, with the DDA not willing to give up land to build the clinics. As a result, only 450 clinics have been built so far instead of the planned 1,000.

While Delhi has some of the biggest hospitals in India, a trip to one of these mega government hospitals can be quite an eye-opener. At the prestigious AIIMS, on any given day, patients and their relatives can be seen lining up for hours before their turn comes to consult with a doctor. In some of the busier sections, such as the emergency room, you can routinely see a queue of gurneys with patients, stretching several hundred metres and snaking its way along the sides of the hospital's long, winding corridors. With more than 9,000 patients visiting every day, the current waiting list for the departments of neurosurgery, ENT and cardiac surgery at AIIMS is two to three years!

This, according to political analysts, was one of the reasons why the mohalla clinics made a positive impact. Jain says that an estimated 50,000 people use the clinics daily and so, by November 2019, over 15 million people had benefited from them.

The mohalla clinic was among the first big interventions announced by the Delhi government. Jain says that the aim was threefold. First, to make available basic healthcare at the local level and to identify any medical problems earlier on, which could possibly be handled with medication. Second, to reduce the burden on the hospitals which were already struggling to cope. And third, by providing timely and free healthcare services, citizens could save money on medical expenses and spend it on goods and services, thereby also giving a boost to the economy.

According to the World Health Organization (WHO), India currently ranks 184 out of 191 nations in terms of gross domestic product (GDP) percentage spending on healthcare. The per capita investment on healthcare by Sri Lanka, China and Thailand is three or four times that of India. The WHO estimates that in 2015, more than 65 per cent of Indians paid for healthcare out of their own pockets since most do not have any health insurance.

To drive home the point, Jain recounts his growing-up days in Delhi. 'My father was a teacher, and while we always had food to eat, we came from a modest home from Delhi's Saraswati Vihar.' Jain says that he often had to share everything with his three siblings while growing up.

'One day, I was coming back from school when a neighbour sitting in my lane loudly remarked, "*Aree chore, dekh tere patlun kahan jaa rahe hain!* (Hey boy, see where your trousers have reached!)". You see, I only had two sets of school clothes and unless clothes were torn, we did not replace them. As a result, over the years while I grew, my trousers stayed the same, coming up above my ankles and closer to my knees.' Jain says that instead of being embarrassed by the taunt of his neighbour, the moment became a turning point in his life. From then on, he swore that he would work to ensure that no school-going child would have to worry about a uniform or affording an education.

Today, a father of two grown-up daughters, Jain says he is proud that AAP's flagship healthcare scheme, modelled around the mohalla clinic, has won international recognition as well. Former UN Secretary-General Ban Ki-moon, who visited the clinics, as well as his predecessor, the late Kofi Annan, have praised mohalla clinics for working towards achieving the WHO's 'universal health coverage goals'. In fact, the former Director-General of WHO, Dr Gro Harlem Brundtland, who was also the former prime minister of Norway, had visited the clinics and was so impressed that she asked the mohalla clinics projects be 'replicated across the country'. For both Kejriwal and Jain, who had accompanied Ban Ki-moon and Brundtland, this was a vindication of their efforts to get the clinics off the ground.

Armed with a good response from the public and big endorsement from the former UN chiefs, the AAP made full use of the international recognition the mohalla clinics were getting.

During the 2020 campaign, the BJP first challenged the AAP in January on the performance of the clinics and the impact they had made. They alleged that the AAP had only built 450 of the 1,000 clinics it had promised and that the facilities at the existing clinics fell woefully short. As proof, BJP's national President, J.P. Nadda released a sting operation video which, he claimed, showed a lack of facilities at the clinics.

The sting operation backfired. As Jain shares, 'The AAP used this and turned it around with the BJP now ending up confirming that the AAP had for a fact built 450 clinics and in the minds of the people, that meant that if the AAP came back to power, it would build the rest.'

While the mohalla clinic was its flagship scheme, the AAP also launched a slew of other schemes including 'Farishtey Dilli Ke'. It is a one-of-a-kind scheme aimed at getting accident victims to the nearest hospital in the fastest possible time. Delhi tops the charts for road-accident deaths in the country. Every five hours, a person is killed on the streets of the capital, according to data from the central Ministry of Road Transport and Highways.

'The chances of survival of an accident victim increase by 70–80 per cent if the person gets to a hospital in the first one hour,' says Piyush Tewari, the chief executive officer (CEO) of the not-for-profit SaveLIFE foundation that he helped set up.

'In the past, often the persons who stopped to help take an accident victim to the hospital [would] end up being regarded as suspects and even [be] hounded by the police,' says Tewari, who adds that this resulted in most people not taking the initiative to inform the police about accident victims on the road for fear of getting involved. 'In case someone calls the police, the victim would have been taken to a hospital without wasting time, but too often, by the time people call for help in critical cases, it's already too late to save a life,' says Tewari.

Jain tells us about the tragic case that led to the creation of Farishtey Dilli Ke. 'There was the case of a fire in Delhi's Gandhi Nagar area in which a man who had heroically saved many lives, died when no hospital took immediate action to admit him and treat him. Instead, he was shifted from hospital to hospital, either because they did not have enough facilities to treat him or they found one reason or another to shift him. The main issue it seems was that they were not sure who would pay for his treatment.'

Farishtey Dilli Ke, which literally means 'angels of Delhi', is a scheme envisaged by Jain to prevent such a situation from happening in the future. It ensures free treatment of any road-accident victim at any private or government hospital. All the expenses are paid for by the Delhi government. It's not just free treatment for the injured person, but the Good Samaritan who brings the accident victim to hospital is also rewarded with ₹2,000 and a certificate.

The scheme is available not just for accident victims, but also for victims of acid attacks and those injured in fires; they too are provided free treatment. If a victim is not satisfied, they can shift to any other hospital of their choice. Up to three such changes are allowed, and the government would foot the bill. On 27 February 2020, following the communal riots of Delhi in which over 50 people lost their lives, the scheme was expanded to also include riot victims.

'Till January 2020, it is estimated that 4,500 people have benefitted from the scheme since it was launched in October 2018,' says Shaleen Mitra, Officer on Special Duty (OSD) to Delhi's Health Minister. He also tells the story of how the scheme presented the humane face of the AAP government in Delhi just before the 2020 Delhi assembly elections. The Delhi government had launched the scheme in October 2019 to provide free treatment in any government or private hospital of the victims of road accidents, fire accidents and acid attack victims.

'One of my relative's friends met with an accident and he had to spend ₹12 lakh on his treatment. I told him about the government scheme, but he did not know about it and the private hospital took advantage of his ignorance. By this time we had already saved 3,000 lives,' says Mitra.

'Then we realized the need to run an awareness campaign about the scheme. The scheme was relaunched. Case studies of survivors were filmed and videographed and a powerful awareness campaign was launched. It had a big impact and the number of people benefitting from the scheme shot up manyfold,' says Mitra. The awareness campaign was launched in October 2019 and it did wonders in creating positivity about the Kejriwal government in Delhi.

'The scheme was very small in terms of the number of

people who had benefitted from it, compared to other schemes of the Delhi government, but its impact was huge. Social media was flooded with positive comments,' adds Jasmine Shah, in-charge of the party's media outreach programme during the elections.

Ticket to Power

Ahead of the 2020 elections, Kejriwal's call to Delhi's women voters was: 'Just like you bear the responsibility of your home, the responsibility of the country and Delhi is also on you. All of you ladies must go and vote and also take the men of your house. Make sure to discuss with the men who the right ones are to vote for.'

Women have formed AAP's strongest voter base through each of its victories in Delhi. While an additional two lakh women turned out to vote in the 2020 assembly elections, a survey conducted by Lokniti-CSDS before the polls had pointed out that women voters gave the AAP a 25 percentage point lead over the BJP.[7] The same survey said that women were 11 percentage points more likely to vote for the AAP than men. In fact, of the 79 women candidates from various parties contesting the 2020 elections, all eight who emerged victorious belong to the AAP. The party had fielded nine women candidates.

Earlier, in its second term, the AAP had provided free water and cheaper electricity. In October 2019, with barely

---

[7]Shreyas Sardesai, 'Stunning Gender Gap: Women Voters Powered AAP's Landslide in Delhi', *The Indian Express*, 15 February 2020. Available at: https://indianexpress.com/article/cities/delhi/stunning-gender-gap-women-voters-powered-aaps-landslide-in-delhi-6267107/, last accessed on 25 July 2020.

three months for the assembly elections, the AAP literally gave women in Delhi a free 'ticket to ride'. Much like *Ticket to Ride*, the popular hit of the 1960s from the iconic band The Beatles, the pink-ticket scheme introduced by the AAP, which allows women to travel for free on the city public transport buses, became an instant hit.

'The cost of providing women free travel on the buses comes to just ₹140 crore a year,' Jain says, providing an interesting comparison by recalling that, in contrast, Gujarat CM Vijay Rupani had purchased an aircraft for his and his officials' use for ₹191 crore. The Gujarat government spent public money on this aircraft, but Kejriwal's government decided to spend ₹140 crore to provide free rides to women, for whom this saving would make a notable difference to their budget. According to Jain, it is a matter of priorities.

Jain points from his office window towards the Yamuna bridge, where a long line of buses has now formed, carrying weary office-goers and factory workers at the end of their shifts, from the city centre towards East Delhi and beyond. 'Close to 4.7 million people use over 7,700 public buses every day in Delhi,' he says. 'For those who own cars, a ₹25 bus ticket may not mean anything, but to a person earning ₹10,000–15,000, it works out to 10 per cent of their monthly income. That's money that they are saving now and can spend on their families, perhaps to even buy school uniforms and trousers for their children,' he says with a big smile.

'The provision of services to the common man was always a part of the pro-poor, pro-*aam aadmi* belief of the AAP and it's in line with that. It's also in line with a pro-women outreach by the AAP. I know that there were many women who would not be able to spend ₹16 or ₹20 for the bus fares, plus the short fares. They would rather walk to work and save the money for their families. This scheme allows women to now use the buses and the Metro, save time and money. It has empowered them more,' says political commentator Neerja Chowdhury. She adds, 'The ordinary person was very happy with this scheme. There were some elite women who had a very elitist response, saying that now the Metro would get more crowded and they would have to share the space. Well, the Metro is meant for them as much as these elitist persons.' Another area she says the government should look at is the last-mile connectivity for families and especially for women, so that they can get to their homes and do so safely.

The pink tickets are doing just that, allowing more women to travel on buses than ever before. According to a survey by the Delhi Transport Corporation (DTC), in just the first month alone since the scheme was launched, ridership by women increased from 32 per cent to 42 per cent, a stark increase of 10 per cent.[8]

Interestingly, while Kejriwal had announced free travel for women on board Delhi's public buses and the Delhi Metro in June 2019, the approval for free ridership on the Metro is still stuck with the Centre. Not wanting to wait, Kejriwal rolled out the scheme for free travel on city buses on 29 October, timing the launch with the festival of Bhai Dooj. Held two days after Diwali, the festival marks the bond between brothers and sisters. It is traditionally celebrated with sisters praying for the long life and well-being of their brothers and brothers showing their care, affection and giving their sisters gifts. The

---

[8]PTI, '10% Rise in Female Commuters in Delhi's Public Buses Since Free-ride Scheme Launch,' *Business Today*, 21 November 2019. Available at: https://www. businesstoday.in/current/economy-politics/10-rise-in-female-commuters-in-delhi-public-buses-since-free-ride-scheme-launch/story/390739.html, last accessed on 5 August 2020.

free-travel scheme launched on the day of Bhai Dooj was—and is—a boon to many women for whom a saving on a ₹20 ticket would mean a lot.

The Big Idea

'Delhiites had by now gotten used to the various schemes. It was as if they felt that the subsidies were the norm and so naturally the question on their mind was, what next?' says Jain.

The feeling in the AAP was that despite various schemes, the party still needed that one big idea that would not only capture the imagination of the voters but also remind citizens of the work done so far. Interestingly, it was the architect-turned-politician Jain who once again came up with what several believe to be the game changer for the AAP in the 2020 Delhi elections.

It was at a meeting at Kejriwal's house to discuss layouts of a newsletter for party workers and volunteers that the subject came around to putting out a bold new thought or idea. While a couple of ideas were discussed, there was nothing that seemed to quite click.

'We will give free power to every resident,' Jain told the gathering. He admits that most people in the room looked puzzled, until finally Kejriwal asked him to explain.

The plan was simple. The AAP first came to power in the capital in 2013 with a promise to halve power rates, but the power distribution and collection of bills was in a shambles. Consumers not only owed over ₹11,000 crore to the power companies, there was a revenue deficit of more than ₹3,500 crore, which meant that the power companies were incurring huge losses in supplying power to customers.

In the five years since 2015, Delhi's power tariff has become the lowest in India. There has been 85 per cent reduction in power cuts compared to 2014. One reason for this was the subsidy that the AAP government was giving on power tariffs, but along with that cheaper power, it had started fixing the transmission and distribution (T&D) systems. This included replacing electro-mechanical power meters with better digital ones to improve earnings. Those customers who had outstanding bills were given a one-time waiver of 25 per cent if they settled their bills. All this led to a sharp reduction in the T&D losses and an improvement in the revenue position of the power distribution companies.

These losses in Delhi had come down to 8 per cent from peak losses of more than 45 per cent of power between 2000 and 2018. Armed with this knowledge, in 2019, the AAP launched its high-voltage election promise, announcing free power for consumers. The condition was that only consumers who consumed less than 200 units of power a month would get a waiver on their monthly bill. A month later, Kejriwal expanded the scheme to include tenants too. Tenants could apply for separate power meters and as long as they consumed less than 200 units a month, they would also get free power.

A shocked BJP and Congress accused the AAP of fooling the people. BJP Delhi leader Manoj Tiwari went a step further and claimed that after the elections, the free power schemes would be withdrawn.

To counter this, the party launched the Kejriwal guarantee card, a list of 10 promises to the city residents, which apart from introducing new schemes such as 24-hour electricity and free travel for students, also reiterated that the free water and power would continue. Kejriwal also took a dig at the BJP, pointing out 'it was alright if a member of Parliament gets

4,000 units of electricity free, but it's a problem if citizens get 200 units free!"[9]

'We had two electricity billing cycles before the elections were due in February,' says Jain. While the Opposition was caught unaware by the announcement and kept insisting that the scheme was too good to be true and would not last, Delhiites started getting their power bills and many of them had zero bills on account of usage below 200 units.

To be sure, the latest subsidy is estimated to cost the government anything between ₹1,700–2,000 crore per year. But interestingly, the AAP government has so far managed to run on a fiscal surplus in 2015–16 and 2017–18. They managed to do so by cutting back on capital expenditure while spending more on education and subsidizing various welfare schemes. While everyone may not agree with the choice of spending, so far the citizens of Delhi seem to be agreeing with Kejriwal.

The 200 units of 'Free Lifeline Electricity' pulled off a miracle. While the BJP and the Congress were still framing their response to the scheme, 32 lakh families, enough to vote a party to power in Delhi, had already received zero electricity bills. The AAP, it seemed, had made the right connection.

---

[9]Press Trust of India, '4,000 Units Free Electricity to MPs Fine, 200 Units to Common Man Not, Asks Kejriwal,' *India Today*, 20 October 2019. Available at: https://www.indiatoday.in/india/story/4-000-units-free-electricity-to-mps-fine-200-units-to-common-man-not-asks-kejriwal-1611332-2019-10-20, last accessed on 25 July 2020.

6

SOCIAL MEDIA

Jantar Mantar

For most Indians, Delhi's Jantar Mantar is synonymous with protests. It's the ideal location, close enough to Parliament and accessed via two main entry and exit points, and readily accessed by the media. For more than two decades, it has been the preferred spot for anyone with a grouse or a cause and wanting to be heard.

It wasn't always so. Before 1993, protests had been largely held at Ramlila Maidan or the Boat Club lawns along Delhi's iconic Rajpath, the road that connects two important monuments, the India Gate and the Rashtrapati Bhavan, the official home of the President of India. But that changed when a massive farmers' agitation led by farmer leader Mahendra Singh Tikait in 1988 laid siege of the Boat Club lawns. It is estimated that over five lakh farmers with bullock carts and cows descended on the lawns and camped there for weeks before the then Congress government led by Rajiv Gandhi relented and agreed to the farmers' demands.

Following the unprecedented turnout, protests were banned at the Boat Club and the closest spot to the Parliament where anyone could protest was Jantar Mantar. And so since

1993, Jantar Mantar came to be *the* protest venue.

It was here that on 5 April 2011 Anna Hazare, a social crusader from Maharashtra, launched his hunger strike demanding a Lokpal, or ombudsman, to fight corruption. This was the first major campaign of IAC, a gathering of individuals and leaders including Hazare, Kejriwal, Supreme Court lawyer Prashant Bhushan and former top cop Kiran Bedi, among others.

It was also where Ankit Lal met his wife.

Lal, who heads AAP's social media team, was at that time a volunteer with IAC, the group organizing and managing the protest. 'You see, I used to stay in Kaushambi, Ghaziabad, and it was only a ₹20 ride away by cycle rickshaw from Arvind's office. So, it was easy for me to quickly hop across from my home to office,' Lal tells us.

Like many others at the time, Lal had first been attracted to the anti-corruption campaign launched by IAC in 2011. Lal had also seen one of Kejriwal's speeches on Facebook and started following the activities of IAC.

The former engineer had been preparing to go to the US to study and possibly pursue a career there, and for this, he had saved up to buy a laptop. 'The fact that I lived near the AAP office, and more importantly, had a laptop, meant that I was tasked with answering official mails for the party and also helping set up its social media page,' Lal tells us.

As the social media in-charge for the AAP, Lal was also on the radar of journalists following the developments in IAC. Prerna Prasad of Network 18 was one such journalist closely tracking the developments of IAC. 'Like a good journalist, Prerna was looking for an inside scoop,' Lal tells us with a big grin. Instead, the two discovered that they both had a lot in common, including a shared belief of wanting to usher in a change in the system and in IAC.

They wanted to take things further and decided to get married. Lal tells us that parents on both sides had been taken aback by the sudden announcement and had reservations. After all, to them, this was far more important that the campaigns they both seemed focused on at that time. Still, the couple persisted and got married on 13 May 2012.

'Both our parents did not come to the wedding and it was Kejriwal who did the *kanyadaan* (the Indian equivalent of giving away the bride),' says Lal. Family members from both sides were not long in reconciling themselves to their marriage, and Lal admits that it was one of his most adventurous and boldest decisions, one which he doesn't regret at all.

That, however, was not Lal's only bold decision. Just four months earlier, in January, Hazare had checked into Medanta hospital in Gurugram, Delhi's satellite city in neighbouring Haryana, after returning from Mumbai, where he had taken ill during a protest. Lal was in the hospital with Hazare when journalist Punya Prasun Bajpai called on Hazare. While Lal says he was outside the room, it was at this meeting that Hazare and Bajpai apparently discussed the formation of a political party.

India Against Corruption was essentially a group of people and it had achieved what it could. One of the big turning points of the campaign happened with Kejriwal splitting from IAC to form a political party in 2012. While several members of IAC went with Kejriwal, there were many who felt that the campaign against corruption should remain apolitical.

This turn of events has been much debated over the years. There have been competing versions of the exact sequence: was it Kejriwal who came up with the idea of forming a political outfit or Hazare or someone else? Bajpai says that it was Hazare who had first asked him how others in IAC felt about forming a political outfit and whether this was the way to proceed. Bajpai had told Hazare that IAC had achieved what it could, but as it wanted to change the political system from within, that would only be possible through a political route. Hazare also seemed convinced and agreed. Bajpai says that when he came out of Hazare's room and informed Kejriwal and others of what Hazare had said, they almost lifted him up on their shoulders and said that he had done the impossible.

Soon after a decision had been taken to form a political party, Kejriwal called Lal and asked him to join and work for the new political outfit full time.

Lal admits that while doing volunteer work for IAC, he had also been preparing for studies abroad. 'I had scored 1290 out of 1300 in my GRE. With this, I had just received an offer for a scholarship to study in the US,' says Lal. With most of his family based in the US, it had been one of Lal's life's ambitions to study and work there. Now with a scholarship in hand, he was torn between what to do. 'Arvind sat down with me and asked me what I really wanted out of life,' Lal tells us. The heart-to-heart talk apparently went on for a few hours, at the end of which Lal was convinced that his work was in India and with the AAP.

'You see, my whole life I had been gearing up for this and my parents were shocked when I told them I was chucking the scholarship to work for the AAP,' says Lal. He adds that while his parents were still trying to talk him out of his decision to join the political outfit, his announcement two months later that he was planning to get married seemed to have helped replace their existing worry with a new one. 'It's as if they had forgotten about my dramatic career move, since now they were anxiously trying to figure out my sudden decision to get married and asked me to take some time to think about it,' he says, chuckling. It is perhaps only befitting and not surprising then that Kejriwal was the one to 'give away the bride' at their wedding.

Changing Media Strategy

A lot had changed since the IAC days—for Lal and for so many others who had taken part in the movement. Now armed with a new purpose in life, Lal set out to build a database of AAP supporters.

While IAC had attracted people from across the country, now a proper database had to be created and maintained. This would be crucial if a fledgling new political party were to have a chance of making its mark.

'You see, in 2011, we did not keep any major database. We largely had details of where the major protests in 700–800 locations across the world were taking place but not details about the people who were attending the meetings or going to protest,' says Lal. India Against Corruption was a Group of People (GoP) and not a political party; the AAP, on the other hand, was a political party that needed to have its people.

So, once again, it was back to Jantar Mantar. After being on hunger strike for 10 days, in August 2012, Kejriwal, Sisodia and Gopal Rai, along with Hazare, announced the formation of a new political party which would continue with the objectives of IAC.

It was also the first time that Lal and his handful of volunteers started regularly uploading updates from the protest site. A database of those attending and a sign-up campaign had also been started to help build a proper database of future voters.

Lal and his team have handled social media for all the elections since the inception of the AAP, and he says that there has been a marked change in both the kind of messaging and the medium of the message.

'In 2012, we did a lot of newspaper interviews and long format interviews,' he says, telling us that it worked as people still had so many questions from them, and that they were still trying to figure out how the party was going to be true to the original idea and goal behind IAC.

Then, in 2013, the AAP started using a lot more graphics to get the main points across. This was going to be the first test for the party, in their first assembly election in Delhi. In 2015, the party started using more pictures and videos; DSLR cameras capable of taking high-resolution pictures and videos were employed at various rallies and meetings to capture key messages from party leaders and workers.

The 2020 elections saw greater use of live-video events, including streaming of rallies and gatherings on Facebook Live and other platforms. 'We have 10,000–15,000 concurrent viewers of the party's live stream at any given time,' Lal tells us. In fact, Facebook Live was first put to maximum use by the AAP during the 2017 Punjab assembly elections.

Unlike advertisements or political messages played out on radio and satellite-based channels, social media is practically free and has an organic network where regular viewers and subscribers of a party's particular feed also help spread the message by forwarding it. This also allows people to send in their comments to and share their thoughts with the political parties.

'A lot of the new technologies come out near the US elections which [were] then available in India,' says Lal. This happened in 2016 when Facebook started rolling out its live broadcast feature to regular users, after initially rolling it out to power users in the US in August the previous year. This allowed the AAP to extensively use Facebook Live during the 2017 Punjab assembly elections.

The big change for the AAP, when it came to social media, happened during the 2019 Lok Sabha polls and the Delhi polls a year later. For the first time, the party advertised on Google and spent close to ₹70 lakh on advertisements on Facebook.

The very fact that artificial intelligence now allows for targeted messaging gave an opportunity to the AAP to create age-specific advertisements for different voter groups across various social media platforms such as Facebook, YouTube and Google.

Up until now, most of the jingles, videos and messaging had been done in-house by volunteers, but for the first time, the AAP hired a professional agency to expand the reach of the party on platforms such as Snapchat, ShareChat and TikTok.

Going into the 2020 elections, the AAP also had a clear advantage. The fact that Kejriwal was its chief ministerial candidate made brand-building and following much easier for the party. Both its rivals, till the end, did not announce a chief ministerial candidate, which experts say cost AAP's opponents heavily.

Both Congress and BJP insiders admit that each party had several contenders and announcing a chief ministerial face could have ended up in partymen working at cross purposes and even sabotaging the elections. Both the Congress and the BJP had witnessed this in 2015, especially the latter, when it parachuted former top cop Kiran Bedi to be its chief ministerial nominee. The last-minute induction of Bedi, along with several leaders from other parties, proved very costly for the BJP in the elections. There was such severe resentment among leaders and workers over fielding rank outsiders, that many party workers reportedly did not even go out to canvass for the official candidate or in some case even worked against the party candidate.

While the BJP and the Congress were on the backfoot without a CM candidate in their campaigns, the AAP did not waste the opportunity to highlight this fact. 'Lage Raho Kejriwal', which translates to 'Keep at it Kejriwal', became AAP's most catchy and effective slogan.

While the AAP concentrated on Twitter and Facebook, where it had a strong presence, its external hired agency was scouring hours of video footage. BJP's Delhi chief was an obvious target, not only because Manoj Tiwari was heading the party, but also because Tiwari, before making his way into politics, had been a popular singer and actor in Bhojpuri films.

'Manoj Tiwari was an obvious choice for memes,' says Lal. Memes or short videos, images, texts or a combination of all three presented in a humorous way, very often top the list of viral content on the internet. There was a lot of video material available, and at one point, Tiwari even threatened to sue the AAP over a meme.[10] This only heightened the interest of mainstream media, which started following the meme wars. According to Lal, 'Putting such memes on television channels would have cost crores, instead now it was happening for free.'

It did not help the BJP that it was still unsure about who could be its CM. Union Minister Hardeep Puri's comment

---

[10]Misha Bhatt, 'BJP Slams AAP, Calls Video Featuring Manoj Tiwari an Attack on Purvanchali Ethos,' RepublicWorld.com, 17 January 2020. Available at: https://www.republicworld.com/india-news/politics/bjp-slams-aap-calls-aapsparody-video-to-be-an-attack-on-bhojpuri-and.html, last accessed on 24 July 2020.

at a function that 'the BJP is headed for victory in Delhi'[11] under Tiwari's leadership sparked off a social media storm and a clarification issued by Puri two hours later on Twitter did little to do damage control. Instead, the AAP used it to jibe the BJP, saying that the party was *'bine dulhe ke baaraat* (a wedding procession without a groom)'.

It is not that only the AAP was using social media to push its message; both the Congress and the BJP had dedicated teams working on social media. The BJP was also reportedly using close to 6,000 WhatsApp groups to seed its message among Delhi's voters. The party had encouraged its workers to start additional WhatsApp groups to spread its message.

In fact, WhatsApp was very effectively used by the BJP in the 2017 UP assembly elections. Like the others, AAP's election team also regularly follows developments, particularly the use of new technology and techniques used by other political entities. One such learning was how WhatsApp can be used as a mass communication tool by the party. Instant, able to carry videos and images easily, and far less expensive than other mediums, WhatsApp is a very effective campaigning tool, and the AAP had learnt this lesson from the BJP. The latter stunned its opponents by its splendid victory in UP, and an analysis of the state election showed that the party had created a powerful WhatsApp network in UP which had played a key role in its victory.

The AAP decided to embrace WhatsApp and started

---

[11]PTI, 'Puri's Statement About BJP Fighting under Tiwari's Leadership Made Choice Very Easy for Delhi People: AAP', *The Times of India*, 24 November 2019. Available at: https://timesofindia.indiatimes.com/city/delhi/puris-statement-about-bjp-fighting-under-tiwaris-leadership-made-choice-very-easy-for-delhi-people-aap/articleshow/72212745.cms, last accessed on 3 July 2020.

using the communication medium in three different ways. First, it connected all its office-bearers and volunteers through WhatsApp. Video, audio, graphics and text messages were created and pushed through these channels, and regular audits were done to test their effectiveness. Volunteers and office-bearers were told to circulate the message they received through the network to all the WhatsApp groups they could.

In a parallel exercise, Vidhan Sabha-wise WhatsApp groups of volunteers were created to quickly disseminate information. This network also underwent an audit to check its effectiveness. The target was to have the network ready six months before the elections.

The effectiveness of the WhatsApp network was impressive not only in sending out communication in real time but also because of its ability to carry a variety of content. It also proved to be a very effective tool to counter propaganda. On several occasions during the 2020 assembly elections, the AAP successfully used its WhatsApp channels to counter propaganda pushed by its opponents at local levels as well as centrally. Counter-messages were being made for each constituency to give a rebuttal to any propaganda message from the Opposition. Another beauty of the medium was that it was equally effective across all socio-economic classes of voters.

The challenge here was threefold: first, creating the network, second, creating the effective content which carried the political message and also had the potential to go viral and third, pushing the content through the network and ensuring its delivery to the target audience. Before electioneering started, AAP's WhatsApp warriors were ready under Ankit Lal.

The exercise, however, took several months of preparation. Meetings were held at the Vidhan Sabha level. Training sessions were organized. A content war room was set up, which rolled out a specified number of videos, audios, graphics and text messages at regular intervals. A studio-like set-up was also created to roll out bulletins and ground reports.

Ghanshyam Kaushik, a former TV journalist, was leading the content team for the WhatsApp network. Kaushik had three tasks at hand. The first was to convey the achievements of the Kejriwal government to the people of Delhi, the second was to counter the hostile mainstream television media and the third was to counter propaganda from the Opposition. Kaushik started rolling out ground reports, vox pops and bulletins, which were an instant hit on WhatsApp. These on-ground reports and bulletins had a very high degree of credibility, which was one of the reasons why this content had a very high potential of going viral.

Thus, following the UP assembly elections and the lessons learnt from the state BJP about the use of WhatsApp, the AAP had formed a well-oiled WhatsApp network of its own to use.

∽

7

PROBLEM-SOLVERS' PARADISE

Pankaj Gupta and Neeraj Gulati have a lot in common. Both are highly successful entrepreneurs. Both have an engineering background which took them to the US, where they did exceedingly well before returning to India. They both also love to solve problems. As key fundraisers, they are both also crucial for the AAP.

'Poll campaign funding is the root cause of corruption,' says Gupta. Dressed in a light-yellow t-shirt, Gupta slightly sinks back into his sofa while stretching both arms behind his head. He pauses, to let that sink in. As national secretary of the AAP and its chief fundraiser, Gupta has often had to perform a tightrope act when it comes to stretching the party's finances.

'During my days as a software engineer, I used to travel frequently to the US. Whenever I met Indians living in the US, they would almost always complain about India. They never spoke proudly about the nation and that made me feel disgusted,' laments Gupta. While this was more than two decades ago, Gupta says that it left a lasting impression on him. 'I realized that they spoke poorly about India and it was all linked to corruption, which was either holding us back or even pulling us back. It's the root cause of all the problems we have today,' he tells us. He adds that tackling corruption will help change the system, and if the system changes, it will also help control corruption.

Gupta started his career with Tata Consulting Services (TCS) and eventually went on to successfully build his own software company which he sold for a small fortune. The experience of creating his own company also taught him how difficult it was to do business in India, especially if you were trying to do a clean deal. 'Even in the private sector, I used to face corruption while dealing with government departments. If you didn't want to pay, there are always others who will gladly work out an under-the-table commission for getting a contract', says Gupta. It was time to either surrender to the system or try and bring about a change.

Long before Gupta came to be one of AAP's key founders and leaders, he had started working with Kejriwal and Sisodia as a volunteer in Parivartan, an NGO which was founded by a group of citizens in Delhi in early 2000. The NGO had been particularly successful in using the Right to Information (RTI) law in Delhi to challenge corruption and help out the ordinary citizen. Interestingly, almost four years before the landmark RTI Act was passed by the Indian Parliament in 2005, Delhi had passed its version of the RTI law. For the first time, there was a comprehensive law which pried open the functioning of more than a hundred government departments in Delhi, which till then had managed to be away from public scrutiny.

At that time, Kejriwal, Sisodia, Gupta and other volunteers of Parivartan started using the RTI to demand answers from various government departments. At the top of their list was the erstwhile MCD. From building and running schools and dispensaries, to making and managing roads and parks, to issuing birth and death certificates, there was little in the lives of Delhi's citizens that the MCD didn't touch. It also had the reputation of being a political battlefield, inefficient and corrupt.

Parivartan started by going after several construction projects, including roads and buildings commissioned by the MCD. The NGO demanded details of how much was being spent. Volunteers would also sit outside government offices, requesting people not to pay bribes to get their jobs done. Next, the group turned its attention to the huge siphoning off of subsidized foodgrains meant for the poor. A widow in East Delhi's Sunder Nagri had approached the group, complaining that she wouldn't get ration or at least never the amount she was entitled to. Using Delhi's RTI Act, Parivartan managed to obtain her ration records which showed that the widow was in fact getting full ration, at least on paper anyway. This was just the tip of a massive scam. Parivartan demanded more details about ration being officially given to other ration-card holders. This was staunchly protested by several ration dealers who took the matter to court, claiming that the information was private as it concerned other citizens.

While a court battle would have taken time and money, Parivartan came up with a solution and asked 300 citizens from the area to file 300 individual RTI petitions seeking details of their own ration and how much they had been getting according to the official records. This time, ration dealers found it difficult to deny the information. The results were scandalous. It was discovered that while 90 per cent of the 300 people had been getting full ration on paper, most had got nothing in reality. A bulk of the subsidized foodgrains meant for the poor and paid for by the taxpayer was being systematically siphoned off through collusion of ration dealers and corrupt officials.

This successful use of the RTI law at the grassroots level

and helping citizens battle corruption catapulted Kejriwal into international limelight and, in 2006, he was awarded the prestigious Ramon Magsaysay Award, given in recognition of integrity in governance and service to the people.

Team Kejriwal had successfully used the system to bring about change. Now that they knew it could be done, it was time to do something bigger.

Activism to Politics

Just as Parivartan had eventually led to the IAC campaign in 2012, the AAP was born out of IAC. 'The moment we decided to go political, I was all for it,' says Gupta.

Having done his stint with Parivartan and seen the changes, Gupta had become increasingly convinced like many others in the AAP that entering the political arena was the only way forward, especially if they sought change on a much larger scale. However, the thing about scaling up is that it also costs money. Determined to show that it was willing to walk the talk on transparency, the AAP announced that it would manage its first political battle, the 2013 Delhi state elections, within a budget of ₹20 crore. The party had arrived at this figure after conducting a survey of how much it would cost to make a serious bid for Delhi.

'We got donations from two lakh people. Some even gave ₹5 and ₹10, others in lakhs,' says Gupta. 'Though the category that gave in lakhs was a much smaller group,' he adds with a chuckle.

This was the first election for the AAP and they went in for crowdfunding. Moreover, the party website kept track of the donations and displayed the total payments received at any given point. The moment it crossed ₹20 crore, the website stopped accepting donations.

Gupta admits that being its first election, the party had perhaps set a lower budget for the polls. He also admits that the other reason was that in case the AAP lost the election, it would not know what to do with the money collected and unspent. 'We weren't political persons and the feeling was that if we did not make a headway in the elections, then politics may not be for us.'

While the AAP had been buoyed by the response IAC had received during public rallies led by Hazare, getting big donors was not that easy at first. 'Amit Agarwal, a non-resident Indian (NRI), was the first person who gave us our first cheque of one hundred thousand dollars,' says Gupta. Agarwal had been a supporter and while his donation was the first big cheque for the party, what was even more important was the message to the voters that people were willing to back the AAP.

A party born out of a movement against corruption was finally netting backers. For the AAP, the contribution from Agarwal was worth a lot more. The party highlighted its first big donation at various political rallies. Several interviews were also lined up with Agarwal, the message being that the AAP was worth it, and to get others to bring out their chequebooks.

Another idea that Gupta came up with was that of organizing group fundraiser dinners for Kejriwal. Such political fundraisers, which can range from a lavish meal with a key political candidate to even a backyard barbecue, are quite common in the US, but it was an innovative step for the AAP. Gupta had spent time in the US, where political campaign financing is at an altogether different level. He, in fact, had attended such a fundraiser, and thought of trying it out for the AAP.

The very first of such fundraiser dinners was held in a hotel in Gurugram. Though, technically, Delhi's satellite city

Gurugram is part of the neighbouring state of Haryana, it was felt that Gurugram had a lot of NRI families. Moreover, a large chunk of people who had lived their whole lives in Delhi had moved to Gurugram following the construction boom, and it was felt that they would still be emotionally connected to the capital city and open to contributing.

The deal was simple: potential donors would be contacted. Those who were keen to attend the fundraiser dinner had to promise a minimum contribution. The hope was that if they were impressed with what they saw, contributors would sign bigger cheques. Gupta says that the party did manage to mop up a decent amount of money while helping build a personal rapport between Kejriwal, donors and influencers.

Interestingly, the ECI sets limits on how much candidates can spend. The aim is to create a level playing field where even those without a big war chest can hope to contest elections and win. But it is interesting that while the ECI sets spending limits on the candidates, there is no limit on how much a party may spend on the election.

The AAP had said that it would contest the Delhi elections with ₹20 crore. It was facing the BJP and the Congress, and was outspent by both its opponents. Gupta admits that, in hindsight, the party could have perhaps collected a little more. As things turned out, the AAP managed to win an impressive 28 of the 69 seats it contested, the BJP emerged as the largest party, while the Congress was humbled and reduced to single digits.

'People give because they believe in something. In 2013, it was a romantic notion about a movement for change. People believed in the movement and Kejriwal and that's why they donated and voted,' says Gupta.

While the first election may have been won on a romantic

notion for change, in 2015, the AAP was facing the tag of being 'bhagoda' (runaway), a reference to its 49-day government which ended in Kejriwal and his Cabinet resigning in Delhi. The AAP had formed a government with the support of the Congress, but Kejriwal said that this was an unworkable relationship. The Opposition was also making the case that the AAP was an experiment run by people who had no idea of how to administer a state.

Even before the 2015 Delhi elections, the mood in the AAP was that of dejection and its volunteer force was largely disheartened. Barely nine months earlier, the AAP had contested 432 seats in the 2014 Lok Sabha polls and had managed to win only four seats.

After the 2014 Lok Sabha polls, there was talk that perhaps people weren't convinced enough to vote for the AAP. The party had done well in 2013, but even then, the voters had still given the BJP more seats. In 2014, it was a sweep for the BJP.

'Show Me the Money'

People were angry with the AAP, the fact that they had resigned and lost an opportunity to work for the people. The AAP worked to explain why it needed to get a bigger mandate from the people, if it was to get a chance at forming the government and bringing about any change. The other task was to convince people to fund the party and its Delhi campaign.

'Show me the money' is perhaps one of the most famous lines in the history of Hollywood. It was made famous by lead actor Tom Cruise, who often repeats these words in the romantic comedy *Jerry Maguire* that released in 1996. Cruise plays the role of a sports agent who is fired for exposing wrongdoings. It is a feel-good film, with audiences rooting for a common person (Maguire) trying to do the right thing when it's easier to go with the tide, even if it means bending the law.

'Another quote that became quite popular from the film was "help me, help you", when Maguire tries to convince his clients to believe in him and convince them that he's giving it all he's got, for them,' says Neeraj Gulati. Also a software engineer, Gulati, like Pankaj Gupta, handles fundraising for the AAP.

'We had to get the successful Indian to fall in love with the messenger and we needed someone they would fall in love with,' says Gulati. 'It was with this sentiment that the AAP started reaching out to its volunteers and voters alike. The AAP had resigned after just 49 days in government, but "it had done so for you!" This was the message the party hoped Delhi's voters would see. "Help me, help you" essentially was the message that the party was sending out to voters.'

In August 2013, Kejriwal had made an emotional appeal to Delhiites that he needed ₹20 crore to contest elections and he had no money. He said that it was the people's responsibility to fuel clean politics with clean money. The appeal left a deep impact on people who had always thought that money was never an issue for a political party. Corruption and politics were so synonymous with each other that people had accepted corruption as a necessary evil in the world of politics. The image of a politician knocking on their doors seeking money to contest election itself became a novelty. 'If they need money, they can't be corrupt' was a parallel that many drew. By making this appeal, Kejriwal made a powerful political statement that he and his party were different from others; by going out and seeking donations, they seemed to be only reinforcing that image.

'The average collection was ₹7 lakh a day and within a short span of time, the party had achieved the target of ₹20 crore,' says Bipul Dey, who was part of the team managing donations. 'I distinctly remember the day when a person sent us a bank draft of ₹50 lakh. We could not believe it. When we spoke to him, we came to know that these were his life savings. He told us that this was the best use of his money that he could think of. We were overwhelmed. When the news broke in the media, it ignited a massive chain reaction,' adds Dey.

While the symbolism of seeking donations to contest elections added to AAP's appeal, Kejriwal went a step further. On the morning of 17 November 2013, he tweeted: 'Our party needed ₹20 crores to fight elections. We have met the target. We don't need any more money for Delhi elections.' This message seemed to further strengthen the people's belief in the party. For not only had they set a target for what it would cost to contest elections and asked for donations, but they were also now announcing that the target had been met and they didn't need more donations. They could have continued accepting more money, but they chose not to. This generated enormous goodwill for Kejriwal and his political start-up. This was a new political norm—a party that was not greedily asking for more, but saying 'thanks, we do not need more.'

The AAP had stolen another march. The hope in the Congress and the BJP camps was that most people, even if they did donate to the party, may not be convinced in the AAP's ability to lead a government and not vote for them. 'They hoped that the enthusiasm on the streets would not convert into votes,' says Manoj Tiwari, a senior journalist and political commentator. But the opinion polls on television were proving them wrong. A party born only a few months ago, with no organizational structure in place and no experience in contesting elections was suddenly the psephologist's dark horse. Opinion polls between September and December predicted the AAP's vote share between 15 and 32 per cent and the number of seats between five and 25. Although the range was very wide, it was certain that this political start-up was set to be a serious disruptor.

Collaborative Solutioning

Most political observers would argue that for the first AAP government, formed in 2013 with external support from the Congress, the writing had been on the wall from day one. The party had come to power by attacking the Congress and its unbroken 15-year rule in Delhi for a string of alleged corruption cases. It was only a matter of time before things came to a head, which they did in 49 days.

With the AAP resigning, the next elections in the state were called only in 2015. During that time, the AAP worked to get the message out to remind people why it had quit and why they needed to support the party once again.

To start with, the AAP started organizing ward- and booth-level meetings with volunteers. This was at the base level to try and keep its volunteer and core voter base intact. Several meetings were also held with various professional groups and the party tried to reach out to voters.

'During the 49-day government, we clearly showed people that we meant business by trying to crack down on corruption and improving governance,' says Gulati. The key was to try and convince the people that they were serious about pursuing this and that people should take a chance on the AAP again.

'The key to getting the message across is also who is giving the message,' says Gulati, who has 13 patents in technology.

'Hard work gets you so far, but it helps [only] if you have good credentials,' he adds. Gulati admits that while hard work helped him in life, the fact that he was enrolled in the prestigious IIT Roorkee often helps open doors and opportunities, and people are generally more receptive. It's another matter that Gulati dropped out of IIT and went to follow his dream of computer engineering.

'We are as much an "innovation engine" as we are a group of people who want to bring about change in politics,' he explains. 'According to NASA, most of north India will not have groundwater within the next decade,' says Gulati. 'Now, how does any government plan to tackle that? What are the solutions? Where will the water come from?'

To tell voters that it was serious about finding solutions to problems, the AAP held a series of webinars or online discussions and seminars. The party would pick an important topic, such as water scarcity, and get an expert from IIT or another leading institution to directly engage and talk with voters. 'This way, people get engaged. They realize that what the expert is saying makes sense and something they should support. The message we convey with these webinars is that, you are not funding a political party but supporting schemes for your own betterment,' says Gulati.

Gulati admits that he got the inspiration for organizing such webinars and linking it to funding from the National Public Radio (NPR) in the US and its funding model. A non-profit public- and private-funded radio syndicate, the NPR on weekends organizes programmes where listeners who are inspired by the broadcasts pledge and donate money to it.

'Take Their Money, But Vote for Us'

'You see, money is needed by a party for campaigning, for rallies and to distribute cash to voters,' says Gulati, adding that the AAP does not distribute cash as freebies to lure voters, but that does not mean that others do the same.

Interestingly, party chief and Delhi CM Kejriwal created a controversy when he asked voters in Goa to accept money that other political parties may offer voters as an inducement for casting their votes, but still vote for the AAP. In fact, Kejriwal, ahead of the 2017 Goa assembly elections, even remarked at election rallies that his party was broke and had no money to campaign for the Goa or Punjab elections.

'The giving of cash, liquor [and] other goodies just before voting time has been growing in the elections,' says political commentator Neerja Chowdhury, adding that 'in the South, families who don't want these allurements also end up taking [them] as they don't want to be identified as non-supporters of any particular party. Hence, they too take. For Kejriwal to openly say that they should take the money was, according to several people, very indiscreet. It was a clever ploy by him when he asked voters to take the money if others were giving and vote for the AAP. By asking voters to do so, he was perhaps helping them overcome the dilemma a voter may have,' Chowdhury says with a laugh.

Gulati, who was also the key in-charge for fundraising in the 2017 Punjab state elections, says that funding can be the easiest of things or a tough challenge depending on how you do your politics. 'Corporates and others traditionally donated money to a political party not so much as they believe in the party's political philosophy but as an insurance to have a sympathetic ear from the party if it gets elected and forms the government,' he says. The problem with that model is that the government is compromised from the very start.

'We want to change that model, we want a citizen-funded model of politics where people give donations to parties because they believe in what the parties are doing,' says Gulati. 'Even if a person were to donate a hundred rupees, we would give that person a receipt. In fact, we would prefer more contributions from such donors as it frees us from money from corporates,' he says.

The other problem, according to Gulati, is that several people would prefer to give cash to the AAP. 'Several potential corporates tell us that if they were to donate to us by cutting a cheque, the government will start harassing them.'

Gulati says that he's not impressed with the introduction of the electoral bonds, which brings about anonymity of the donors. Introduced by the National Democratic Alliance (NDA)-led government in 2017–18, any individual or corporate can buy electoral bonds ranging from ₹1,000 to ₹1 crore from select branches of the State Bank of India (SBI). The name of the purchaser is kept confidential and the corporate or individual can then give these bonds to fully registered political parties which can encash them.

Interestingly, before the electoral bonds were introduced, election rules allowed parties to not disclose names of donors if the amount received from the donor was less than ₹20,000. Several parties used this to claim that most of their supporters had donated less than ₹20,000. But with the introduction of the electoral bonds, the cash limit from each donor has been reduced to ₹20,000. For a bigger donation, the party will have to share details of the donors with the ECI.

The scheme has kicked up a controversy. While the NDA government claims that by using electoral bonds corporates and individuals can donate to political parties through a legal banking channel, the Reserve Bank of India (RBI), India's central banker, and the ECI have told the Supreme Court of India that the funding by electoral bonds hides the identity of the donor and has made the system more opaque. In fact, the Communist Party of India (Marxist) (CPI[M]) and the NGO Common Cause along with the Association of Democratic Reforms (ADR), a non-profit which works on electoral reforms, have petitioned India's top court against the scheme on the grounds that the scheme needs to be transparent.

While petitioners have asked for the scheme to be suspended till the case is fully heard, the court has so far decided to continue hearing the case but has not suspended the sale of the controversial bonds.

The AAP has also opposed the scheme from the beginning, claiming that it will lead to anonymous funding of elections and benefit the ruling party. Interestingly, just before the 2020 Delhi elections, ₹81.67 crore of electoral bonds were purchased to be given to political parties ahead of the elections. The main beneficiaries of these bonds are not known.[12]

An RTI query filed by retired naval officer Lokesh Batra reveals that between 13 January and 22 January 2020, the largest number of the bonds were sold by the SBI's Kolkata branch. Seventy-eight of these bonds were of ₹1 crore, while 34 of them were of ₹10 lakh. No denominations of ₹1,000 or ₹10,000 were sold.

While the recipients of the bonds sold ahead of the Delhi

[12]Priscilla Jebaraj, '₹81.67 Crore Worth Electoral Bonds Sold Before Delhi Polls, Says Response to RTI Query', *The Hindu*, 13 February 2020. Available at https://www.thehindu.com/news/national/8167-cr-worth-electoral-bonds-sold-before-delhi-polls-rti-query-shows/article30804578.ece, last accessed on 5 August 2020.

elections are not known, an analysis of the 2018–19 accounts of major political parties by ADR shows that the BJP has been the biggest beneficiary of these bonds. During 2017–18, 95 per cent of the bonds purchased went to the BJP, according to the ADR.

'The biggest problem of a democracy is the financing of elections. It's like the Gangotri; if the source gets polluted, then the whole river is polluted and compromised,' says Gulati.

So, is the whole system of electoral funding in India still compromised? As with several other important public issues in India, it is going to be up to the apex court to decide.

ᔓ

8

BATTLE LINES

The year was 2013, the month, July. The sky over Delhi was generally cloudy and 12 rainy days had been forecast for the capital that month. While temperatures had dropped after a very hot spell in June and had been replaced by high humidity, touching 49 per cent, the political temperature was soaring in the capital city. It was like an initial public offering (IPO) at the stock exchange. There was a lot of buzz about the AAP and this group of young disruptors, but people were not sure how much political space they would be able to make for themselves. Would they rise or would they crash? Delhi had been the epicentre of the high-voltage anti-corruption movement led by the Magsaysay Award-winner and Gandhian, Anna Hazare. Now Arvind Kejriwal, the 45-year-old bureaucrat-turned-activist-turned-politician, who had played a key role in the nationwide agitation, was staking claim to the throne of Delhi. He had emerged as a prominent public figure with immense goodwill and promise.

In this unusual but nail-biting game of political *shatranj* (chess) in 2013, there were three players facing each other. The Congress was playing to defend its bastion. Against the backdrop of the anti-corruption stir, the BJP had smelled blood and was playing the challenger. And the third was Kejriwal and his team, facing the two shrewd players who knew every trick in the book. While the two preferred to wait and watch, Kejriwal, with nothing to lose, decided to make the first move in the game that saw sworn rivals seeming to gang up. The supposed opponents switched sides and became strange bedfellows. The next few months saw a script rolling out in the power corridors of Delhi that would give any Bollywood thriller a run for its money.

The game had begun. Kejriwal took the lead by announcing his candidature from the prestigious New Delhi seat, directly challenging the then CM Sheila Dikshit, who had been invincible for the last 15 years. He also challenged the BJP to field its chief ministerial candidate from the same constituency.

Kejriwal told Delhi's voters that 'politics of convenience must end'. In the midst of traditional politics, where political leaders who till yesterday had sworn to live and die by a certain ideology switch sides without skipping a heartbeat, Kejriwal and AAP's message and politics seemed like a breath of fresh air in New Delhi's power circles. The messaging was simple, direct, fresh and newsy. The media also picked it up.

The 2013 elections turned into a media spectacle. AAP's list of candidates comprised civil services aspirants, trainee journalists, engineers, professionals and professors. Most of them had never been in politics. This further added to the mystique and freshness of the new political start-up. Kejriwal and his team became the new media darlings and even before the veterans in the BJP and the Congress seemed to realize, round one had already gone to the AAP. TV screens were flooded with the young, fresh faces of professionals-turned-politicians, and the people of Delhi could relate to them.

By the end of the second term of the UPA-led coalition government at the Centre, citizens were fed up of the vitiated atmosphere. A sense of hopelessness seemed to have descended. The central government seemed to be locked in policy paralysis, apparently not taking any strong decisions or sending out a clear message. News reports of scams and exposés of alleged corruption in allotment of coal blocks or the auction of spectrum of air waves to telecommunication companies further added to a feeling of despondency and anger. Both these cases revived memories of the 2010 Commonwealth Games in Delhi and the string of corruption cases under investigation. A lot of that anger was directed at the Congress, which was in power both at the Centre and in Delhi, where it had ruled for 10 and 15 years, respectively. The anger coupled with anti-incumbency, further created the conditions for a change in the political leadership at the Centre.

While changing a system that was deeply entrenched over decades would take a tsunami, the arrival of the AAP on the scene in Delhi, riding on the back of Hazare's IAC movement, brought with it a feeling of the fresh air of 'new politics'. It seemed as if it was the beginning of the end of conventional politics.

The AAP had another advantage; its leaders—almost all from non-political backgrounds—started reaching out and literally knocking on doors, seeking a vote for the party. While the BJP and the Congress fell back on their tried-and-tested party spokespersons and political leaders, AAP's volunteers and leaders seemed to offer a fresh start and a hope for cleaner politics. For a cosmopolitan city such as Delhi, it was a new and welcome idea. This was the launch pad for the AAP in its first election.

The AAP had managed to convince the voter to give them a chance. In the very first electoral battle in 2013, as the results came in, the BJP and the Congress quickly realized that the real game was to be played now. The former had won 32 seats with its ally SAD contributing one to its tally, four short of the majority mark in a House of 70. The Congress had won only eight, while the AAP with 28 seats was the biggest stunner. But the riddle was to work out numbers to form the government.

Armed with experience, both the BJP and the Congress perhaps knew better that whoever formed the government, it would be a short-lived one. No one also wanted another election right away. It seemed that both parties prepared their strategies to kill two birds with one stone. To both the BJP and the Congress, Kejriwal had been a monkey on the shoulder, one they would happily remove from the equation. While Kejriwal, true to his form, had followed the disruptor model of a political start-up, both national parties had the political acumen and experience from the past, something they were banking on. In the past, both the big parties had strategically helped to form short-lived governments with predictable fallibility given the strains of uncommon goals.

BJP's chief ministerial candidate, Dr Harsh Vardhan appeared before the media after meeting Delhi's Lt Governor Najeeb Jung. Harsh Vardhan described how his party believed in transparency and value-based politics. He said his party was short of a majority and thus, despite being the single largest party in the House, would choose to sit in the Opposition.

After the BJP, Lt Governor Najeeb Jung invited the AAP to form the government. By that time, Kejriwal and his team had understood that there was a feeling among a large section of voters, who had voted for the BJP or the Congress, that they had missed the opportunity to vote Kejriwal and his team of young revolutionaries to power. These voters were favourable towards the AAP but had not voted for it because they had never thought that the party could make it this close to the majority mark. Sensing this mood, Kejriwal did not outright decline the offer of the Lt Governor and instead wrote letters to the top leadership of the BJP and the Congress.

To accept the invitation of the Lt Governor and try to form the government had its own risks, especially as the AAP did not have the numbers by itself to form the government. Not taking the risk would be seen as running away by the voters. Could the AAP reduce the risk? Kejriwal crafted a cleverly worded letter to both the BJP and the Congress. In it, he listed out 18 issues. Not wanting to take the blame of a re-election, Kejriwal gave an option to both, that if they were ready to accept AAP's agenda on these 18 issues, the party was ready to assume power in Delhi.

While the BJP did not reply to the letter, its senior leader Arun Jaitley wrote a blog on 9 December saying that the Congress should extend its support to the AAP and help it form the government. The Congress was also quick to accept 16 of the 18 agenda points put forth by the AAP. On 14 December, BJP leader Dr Harsh Vardhan also made a statement that the AAP should form the government with the support of the Congress party.

It was an untenable situation before the AAP. The Lt Governor had invited it to form the government, the BJP was repeatedly saying that the AAP must form the government with the support of the Congress, which had agreed to 16 out of its 18 demands. Still not entirely convinced and worried about the political consequences, either way, Kejriwal turned to Delhi's voters once again and said he would take people's opinion on whether the AAP should form the government in Delhi or not.

The AAP organized a referendum. It sought people's vote on whether it should form the government or not through text messages on mobile phones, emails and via public meetings. A majority of those who responded seemed to support the decision to form a government. Armed with this mandate, Kejriwal accepted the Lt Governor's invitation to form a minority government in Delhi. On 28 December 2013, Kejriwal took oath as the seventh CM of Delhi. He was the second-youngest CM of Delhi and was leading Delhi's youngest Cabinet ever.

As political pundits had predicted, the government was to be short-lived, though its life turned out to be much shorter than most predictions. It seemed as if it was a government in a hurry. Kejriwal and his ministers were the new TV superstars. Good or bad, his ministers were earning high TRPs (Television Rating Points). The government was being run on TV. There was no dearth of stories as the entire country watched the Kejriwal-starrer reality TV show. Almost every aspect, starting with the oath ceremony which was held in the presence of a huge Delhi crowd in Ramlila Maidan, to the thousands of Delhiites who thronged Kejriwal's daily Janata Darbar, everything was seemingly being captured by TV cameras and played out on screens across the country. The arrest of government staffers accused of corruption and caught on sting operations carried out by common people, registering of first information reports (FIRs) against the country's biggest industrialists and union Cabinet ministers, all added to the high-voltage news stories which continued to break all-time TRP records. However, AAP's high-voltage story came to an end with Kejriwal resigning as the CM after an emotional speech in the Delhi Assembly 49 days after his swearing-in.

To political observers, it seemed as if Kejriwal had resigned because he did not want to give an opportunity to the bigger parties to vote him out and to pull the plug. It had been a short-lived government, but the AAP had managed to start off with several of its promises and, importantly, this had also been amplified by the media.

Kejriwal may have left the government, but he managed to stay on in the political game. Now he was asking voters that unless he got a full mandate, he could not work or deliver on promises. Kejriwal had taken a big gamble and it was going to pay off.

From Challenger to Defender

After the 2013 elections, Kejriwal had only earned the eligibility to face the grandmasters in the battle of chess. The real test of his political acumen, reflexes and instinct was to mature in 2015. The conquest for the capital of the nation was between him and BJP's political grandmaster of his times, Amit Shah.

Even before the game started, it was advantage Amit Shah playing White. The right to choose the time of elections lay with him. Though the throne belonged to Kejriwal, for the audience and for all practical rules of the game, he could only earn the status of the challenger, and not the defender.

The siege was laid, and after every move, the noose around Kejriwal's neck was tightening. He chose to open with the famous 'King's Gambit' and tried cornering the strong opponent on the issue of leadership—let the BJP name its chief ministerial candidate, he demanded. The BJP had no local leader to match Kejriwal. While the game seemed to be tilted in BJP's favour in 2013, in 2015, the BJP had so far not projected a chief ministerial face. That was until Shah pulled out a surprise, fielding the BJP's queen, Kiran Bedi, right in the middle of the chessboard.

To many political observers, this was the master move.

Bedi, a former top cop, had many positives on her report card. As the first senior woman police officer, Bedi had earned the respect of many when under her, the Delhi Traffic Police towed away the wrongly parked car of the then Prime Minister of India, Indira Gandhi, in August 1982. This earned Bedi the nickname 'Crane Bedi', in reference to the towing cranes used by the Delhi Police. She also had a clean record and reputation and so, Kejriwal could no longer claim to be the only one leading a campaign for clean politics.

Bedi also had everything that Kejriwal had—or rather, she had even better credentials. If Kejriwal was an Indian Revenue Service (IRS) officer, Bedi was an Indian Police Service (IPS) officer. She was a far more celebrated civil servant than Kejriwal. Like the AAP chief, Bedi, too, was a Magsaysay awardee and she, too, had been an important part of Hazare's agitation. Not just that, in the 2013 elections, Kejriwal and AAP leaders had themselves approached Bedi to lead the party and become its chief ministerial candidate in the Delhi elections, but she had refused. This move by the BJP put the AAP in a quandary. The AAP was now finding it difficult to even criticize Bedi. This move by the BJP seemed to have checkmated the Kejriwal team.

Delhi in the past had also voted Congress leader Sheila Dikshit back to power three consecutive times as CM. A woman contender as CM seemed like a winning bet for the BJP. Could the game be over in a few moves?

The BJP strategist had, however, not taken into account an important outcome of parachuting Bedi into lead position. The cadre-based party was shaken by Bedi's lateral entry and soon it was apparent that they were rejecting this move and would not lend their support. The heavyweight Bedi very soon became a dead weight as the cadre turned against their own party candidate. According to poll analysts, they instead lent support to AAP candidates, to ensure that the BJP did not win elections under Bedi's leadership.

In a stunning verdict, Kejriwal and the AAP, still in its infancy, won a record 67 out of 70 seats. The novice had managed to beat the great grandmaster of the BJP 67–3. The party, which only two years ago had been the single largest party in Delhi, planned to avenge itself.

The Final Encounter

Chess, they say, is a finely honed game between two well-matched strategists, and no two games can ever be the same. In 2020, it was once again the AAP and the BJP going head to head. But this time, Kejriwal was playing White, as a clear defender.

The chief architect of BJP's political strategy, Shah was on the other side, this time as the challenger. But it was advantage Black. On 9 November 2019, the Supreme Court delivered its judgement on the Ram Janmabhoomi–Babri Masjid land dispute case, with the top court paving the way for the construction of a Ram temple at the disputed site in Ayodhya, and ordering an alternate five acre plot of land to be provided for building a masjid. The judgement was a shot in the arm for the BJP which, since 1996, had made building the Ram temple in Ayodhya one of its key promises. In Jammu and Kashmir, Article 370 and Article 35A had been abrogated, ending the special status that the state had enjoyed so far. Both the decisions were tectonic shifts and while many cheered the decisions, the BJP believed that the voters of Delhi would show their gratitude in the Delhi polls as well.

That confidence was further emboldened when the BJP

won the 2019 Lok Sabha polls by a thumping majority; they even termed it 'winning momentum'. At the same time, the AAP had faced its worst defeat ever in Delhi in the same election. It also had the burden of incumbency, having governed Delhi for a full five-year term and the government to be judged for its work.

History favoured the BJP. Though some ruling parties had won elections in the past, they had not done so by showcasing their work. The performance of the government had only been a baggage to carry along. So, BJP's calculation was straight arithmetic and it seemed to be a cakewalk for them. Though the picture for the BJP seemed to be very bright, several of the challenges that had haunted the party in the first election were staring it in its face once again.

The first challenge was that once again, Kejriwal was daring the BJP to name its chief ministerial candidate for Delhi. To up the ante, Kejriwal launched a new strategy that took BJP's strategists by surprise. Using the ubiquitous city autorickshaws, a poster campaign was launched. The autorickshaws started carrying a poster with two pictures—Kejriwal on one side and BJP leader Vijay Goel on the other, in a face-off with each other. The poster posed a straight question to Delhiites: 'Who would they like to choose as their CM?'

While Goel, a Rajya Sabha MP and former Delhi BJP state president, had not been seen as a frontrunner for the CM's post, it helped the AAP underscore the fact that the BJP had not announced its CM candidate. BJP's plan was to extend the strategy used in the national elections and it was pitching PM Modi against Kejriwal.

The stakes for the 2020 Delhi elections were high and the former BJP President and Union Home Minister Amit Shah took control of the state's elections.

In a chat with one of the authors before the 2020 elections, noted social science scholar and a professor at the Centre for the Study of Developing Societies (CSDS), Delhi, Abhay Dubey predicted that the AAP stood a very good chance to win the Delhi assembly elections. 'You should win for the very reasons that were behind BJP's resounding victory in the 2019 Lok Sabha elections. In those elections, the Opposition failed to offer a leader who could match Modi's stature and standing. The Opposition thought that there was a silent but strong anti-incumbency against the NDA government, which was actually not the case,' Dubey said. 'This is the same for Kejriwal's government in Delhi. The Opposition does not have any credible leader who can match his stature and standing. Also forget anti-incumbency, this government has earned immense goodwill and there is a strong pro-incumbency wave in its favour,' he added.

Listening exercises carried out at different levels by the AAP had also pointed in the same direction. From the strategy point of view, the AAP was clear that the campaign would have a two-pronged approach: cornering opponents on the issue of leadership and keeping the central discourse of elections around the performance of the government in the last five years.

Kejriwal once again tried to corner the BJP on announcing its chief ministerial candidate. Amit Shah refused to engage in that debate. While there were several potential CM candidates, including BJP Rajya Sabha MP and Union Minister Vijay Goel, Lok Sabha MP and the party's Delhi unit President Manoj Tiwari, Union Health Minister Dr Harsh Vardhan and cricketer-turned-politician and BJP's Lok Sabha MP from Delhi Gautam Gambhir, none of them was named as the CM candidate. The BJP leaders were seen to be running their own campaigns and speaking in different languages.

Kejriwal and his team had one agenda: to keep reminding people of the services provided by the AAP government. Initially, the BJP was forced to try and corner the AAP on these grounds. Several of the AAP government's flagship programmes came in for attack, from CCTV cameras in the city to improved city schools and mohalla clinics. BJP's attack on AAP's developmental track record seemed to have a flaw. The more the BJP raised these issues, not only was the AAP successfully able to respond, but by raising the issue, the BJP was helping put the focus on developmental work, which was exactly what the AAP had wanted. The AAP was managing to keep the issues local and totally focused on development.

When Shah dismissed AAP's flagship mohalla clinics as non-starter and useless, the fact was that by September 2019, more than 16 million people were estimated to have already directly benefitted from these clinics which provided primary healthcare, medicines and diagnostic tests at their doorstep, that too for free.[13] BJP's high-pitched campaign against the clinics not only fell flat, it also dented its credibility among those who had benefitted first hand.

The BJP made another tactical error. In an attempt to take the focus away from the 'Kejriwal vs who?' campaign and bring it back to 'Modi vs Kejriwal', their strategists felt that if they succeeded in bringing the discourse back to the latter, they would easily succeed in getting votes. PM Modi had, after all, navigated the BJP to its historic second term with an even bigger majority in the Lok Sabha.

---

[13]HT Correspondent, 'Mohalla Clinics Served 16.24 Million People in Four Years: Delhi Health Minister', *Hindustan Times*, 6 September 2019. Available at: https://www.hindustantimes.com/delhi-news/mohalla-clinics-served-16-24-million-people-in-four-years-delhi-health-minister/story-vWd7XwyYW9NEIcf6uGnUeM.html, last accessed on 5 August 2020.

At an election rally on 4 February 2020, PM Modi while addressing the audience said, 'The government in Delhi does not care about the lives of the people living here. What is the fault of the homeless who are not allowed to get homes under the Pradhan Mantri Awas Yojana (PMAY)? What is the fault of farmers that they do not get benefits under the PM-Kisan Samman Nidhi? Why did daily commuters have to suffer because the fourth stage of Delhi Metro expansion was not given clearance (by city government) for two years?'[14] The PM's reference was to several projects, either by the central government or in a large part funded by the central government, being stuck because of the Kejriwal government.

Just a few months before the PM's rally speech and the assembly elections, during the 2019 campaign for Lok Sabha elections, one of the main campaign slogans of the BJP had been '*Modi hai toh mumkin hai* (If there's Modi, it's possible)'. Without even saying it, to most, it was obvious that the BJP was referring to the decisive action and decisions of the Modi government, led by the PM, who could turn the impossible into possible. Whether it was the surgical strike on the launching pads of terrorist camps inside Pakistan or the abrogation of Article 35A and Article 370 of the Constitution, these were all presented as manifestations of a PM who could get things done.

Ironically, now ahead of the assembly elections, in stark contrast to this macho, can-do image of the PM, BJP strategists and script writers made the PM himself admit that while he wanted to do something for the people of Delhi, it was Kejriwal

---

[14]Moushumi Das Gupta, 'Kejriwal Has Kept Delhi's Poor Away from Central Schemes. This Is How Voters Feel about It,' *The Print*, 7 February 2020. Available at: https://theprint.in/politics/kejriwal-has-kept-delhis-poor-away-from-central-schemes-this-is-how-voters-feel-about-it/360742/, last accessed on 27 July 2020.

who was not allowing him to do so. After the PM's speech, BJP party spokespersons also took the lead in blaming Kejriwal in high-decibel TV shows for not allowing PM Modi to do what he wanted to for the welfare of the people.

This campaign not only fell flat but actually boomeranged on the BJP. Were they saying that PM Modi, who had already managed to do the impossible, had been checkmated by Kejriwal? Also, each time BJP spokespersons brought up the schemes which they claimed had been stalled by the AAP, it gave AAP spokespersons the opportunity to showcase how the schemes introduced by the Kejriwal government were already delivering services to the people.

With the BJP failing to get the required traction on its attack on AAP's development report card, several BJP leaders started trying to corner the AAP on issues such as Shaheen Bagh and the CAA. The final round of the Delhi elections would be among the most bitter, divisive and vitriolic the city has seen so far.

∽

9

POLITICAL TRAPS

The Game of the Century

It was a pleasant evening, the kind where one might need a light jacket if stepping out. But the 13-year-old schoolboy from Brooklyn was sweating as he rushed through the thick pile of leaves that had been gathering on the ground like pools of water after a good spell of rain. It was 17 October 1956 and as the boy rushed to the Marshall Chess Club, he could hear his heart pounding as it tried not to betray the pace of his feet and hide his anxiety about what was to come next.

As he entered the red-carpeted staircase leading to the club's lobby tournament hall, he was greeted by his opponent of the day, Donald Byrne, an international master and a former US Open Champion. A 25-year-old dark-haired elegant player, Byrne had defeated Samuel Reshevsky, the strongest American grandmaster, in his last game and was on his way to win the Rosenwald Memorial Invitational Tournament. It was the seventh round of the tournament, and it looked like a cakewalk for Byrne. The 13-year-old Robert James Fischer was a nobody in the chess world. For Byrne, with his past record, his reputation as a very aggressive player and his immediate victory over Reshevsky, the outcome of the next game was a foregone conclusion.

The next five hours saw an unbelievable nail-biter. Fischer sacrificed his queen, considered the most powerful piece in chess. The experienced master Byrne walked right into his trap and lost the game. The individual who was a nobody then, but would go on to become a world champion, had just outsmarted a grandmaster and stunned the world.

Hans Kmoch, the arbiter of the game and a noted theoretician of his time, made a remark that is still engraved in the history of the chess world: '[A] stunning masterpiece of combination play performed by a boy of 13 against a formidable opponent, matches the finest on record in the history of chess prodigies. Bobby Fischer's [performance] sparkles with stupendous originality.' Kmoch also called it the 'Game of the Century'.

Sixty-four years later, in a political match between a national heavyweight and a comparative novice, a parallel to the Bobby Fischer match came to mind. When Kejriwal turned the tables on BJP's chief political strategist and Chanakya, Amit Shah in the 2020 assembly elections, many watched with their mouths agape.

To be sure, the political chessboard opened with Shah controlling the central squares of the board which saw a high-decibel communal campaign. However, he ended up being pushed to the edges of the board just as it seemed that he was only a few moves away from catching Kejriwal in a checkmate!

Noted social scientist and director of Indian Languages Programme (ILP) at CSDS, Abhay Kumar, who keenly follows Indian politics, says, 'It was the most communal election ever fought in the history of independent India. It surpassed communal election campaigns after the 1966 Anti-cow

Slaughter Agitation and Babri Masjid demolition in 1992.' He further adds that 'it was a firmly grounded AAP and its very successful model of governance that saved the election for Kejriwal.'

The Midnight Call

Ratnesh Gupta was a share broker and, like many others in his profession, he understood the risks the bourses bring. But he also knows that the higher the risk, the higher the reward or the bigger the failure: it is about taking a chance.

That's what he did in 2012. Gupta, like many others, had been attracted to the IAC campaign launched by Hazare. 'I always dreamt of a corruption-free India. In 2011, when Hazare launched his anti-corruption movement, I was also attracted to it. Suddenly, I found myself a part of the agitation. I was there on the day the AAP was formed. I also became a founder member of the party. Then came elections. There was no organization, no experience to contest elections, no funds. Manish Sisodia was contesting from Patparganj. There were very few volunteers. I have very fond memories of the first campaign,' Gupta recalls.

The former share broker found himself walking along with Sisodia in the streets of Patparganj, managing his election campaign in 2013. 'It all happened like a Bollywood film. I can never forget the taste of that victory. It seemed as if the purpose of this life has been achieved,' says Gupta.

Sisodia is Delhi's Deputy CM and Kejriwal's second-in-command. As one of the most visible members of the AAP and as Deputy CM, Sisodia's 2020 re-election did not seem to be a tough contest, and that was almost his undoing.

The first one to spot trouble was Gupta and he too

stumbled on it by chance. As someone who has been a key part of Sisodia's campaign from Delhi's Patparganj constituency, Gupta had built a strong network of locals. 'I was having a casual conversation with a young boy when he told me of an interesting job that he had secured with a foundation. When I enquired further, he revealed that the job assigned to him was to identify crowded chatter points such as local tea stalls, Mother Dairy booths, paan shops, etc., mingle with locals and start conversations with them. He had been instructed to hold street discussions on given lines and share videos given to them.' This alerted Gupta, who started making inquiries from his other contacts about this 'foundation' and what it was doing.

He soon realized that that this young boy from his neighbourhood was not alone and there were several others who had been recruited by the 'foundation'.

'I soon realized that the BJP and the RSS were investing heavily in a temporary network of local youngsters and retired people to push their propaganda in Sisodia's constituency,' Gupta tells us. 'Some of my local acquaintances are RSS volunteers. Just a few days before elections, one of such contacts alerted me. He told me that the RSS was working on a "Giant Killer plan",' he further adds.

The idea was to target the senior-most AAP leaders in their own constituencies. It seemed that the political opponents were working on tailor-made local strategy for targeting AAP's top leadership, including Sisodia. 'Manish ji was one such target. He was the mascot of Kejriwal's model of governance. His defeat would not have been just the loss of one seat, but would have been a moral defeat for Kejriwal,' says Gupta.

Gupta was baffled by these developments, and put all of them together to make sense of the sequence, but the worst was yet to come. 'It was just one day before the nominations for candidature were to close. Around 11 p.m., I received a call from the New Delhi constituency, from where CM Kejriwal himself was contesting. The tip-off was mind-boggling. The caller, an old well-wisher of the party, informed me that prominent Valmiki leader Cheena Maharaj was switching sides and could contest against Kejriwal on a BJP ticket. It was very difficult to believe,' shares Gupta.

It took Gupta a minute to come to terms with the new reality and its political implications. As a party leader who coordinated with the Safai Karmchari (sanitation workers') union, Gupta, more than anyone else, understood the importance of Maharaj in the election battle for the prestigious New Delhi seat.

To make this point, Gupta recalls the time when the AAP had just been formed. 'It was born in Delhi, so the idea was to launch it with a puja at the historical Valmiki Mandir at Mandir Marg in the capital,' Gupta tells us.

Valmiki Mandir has a huge historical and symbolic significance, especially for the AAP. Mahatma Gandhi had stayed at Valmiki Mandir when in Delhi and used to teach children there. As sanitation workers, the members of the Valmiki community were considered to be from the lower castes and Gandhi, who had championed the cause of social upliftment, had chosen to stay at the *basti* to send out a message.

The election symbol of the AAP is the broom, and Valmiki Mandir seemed to be the apt place for the launch of AAP's debut political campaign for the 2013 assembly elections. The problem for Kejriwal and the AAP was that a majority of the Valmiki community in the area had traditionally been supporters of the Congress party.

When Kejriwal launched his political campaign in 2013 at the Valmiki Mandir, some of the residents of the area had opposed his entry into the temple with his supporters. It was Maharaj, a respected elder of the community and also the chief priest at the temple, who persuaded his community. Maharaj had also wholeheartedly supported Kejriwal and had even performed a puja for his success in the political battle at the temple. Maharaj's support was very crucial for the party to make inroads into the community, and as a result of his support and the response from the Valmiki community, the AAP had managed to win nine out of 12 seats reserved for Dalits in the debut 2013 elections. In 2015, it was a clean sweep, when it won all 12 reserved seats.

When the AAP announced its Scheduled Caste (SC)/ Scheduled Tribes (ST) wing, Maharaj was made the chief patron of the body. Kejriwal had even remarked on the occasion, 'Cheena Maharaj is like our guru and with his blessings we shall take the organization forward.'[15] This priest of the 150-year-old temple had a very good hold over his community and helped Kejriwal in the initial days of the party.

Now, almost seven years later, Gupta realized that the AAP was about to lose the support of a crucial figure ahead of an important political campaign. Gupta recalls that after getting news of Maharaj being ready to switch sides, he spent the next few minutes calling his contacts in Valmiki Basti, from where Maharaj still operated. These calls only confirmed his suspicion. The contacts in the area confirmed that Maharaj had been hobnobbing with BJP leaders and was planning to file his nomination from the New Delhi seat on a BJP ticket.

---

[15]Dipankar Ghose, 'Next on AAP's Charm List: Wooing Delhi's Dalits,' *The Indian Express*, 5 December 2014. Available at: https://indianexpress.com/ article/cities/delhi/next-on-aaps-charm-list-delhis-dalits/, last accessed on 24 July 2020.

Around midnight that night, Gupta called Kejriwal. He gave the party chief a detailed account of what he had heard from his sources. Kejriwal immediately rushed a senior party leader to Cheena Maharaj. What we know now is that Maharaj did not enter the poll fray on a BJP ticket, but joined the Congress soon after.

Kejriwal's troubleshooters were quick to make up for the loss. Another prominent leader of the community, Sanjay Gehlot, quit the BJP and joined the AAP. Kejriwal comfortably won the seat by a margin of 21,697 votes, though his victory margin was reduced by close to 10,000 votes.

The Queen's Sacrifice

'It was carpet bombing in typical RSS style. By my estimate, some 10,000 to 12,000 people had been pressed into the job in Sisodia's constituency Patparganj in a single day, to create a propaganda buzz,' says Sheetal P. Singh, a former journalist and a political observer who has been tracking political campaigns as a hobby for many years now.

Singh says that he, along with four of his friends, drove to Patparganj to get a feel of the ground situation. 'What we found was astounding. The ground situation was starkly opposite to what was being talked about in the political circles or was being written about in the newspapers. While the AAP had never flagged Sisodia's seat as vulnerable, the BJP had a clear edge over Sisodia on the ground. Our calculation was that both the BJP and the Congress had picked up Pahari (from the hills) candidates, which would benefit Sisodia. But when we started talking to people in the constituency, we soon realized that the Congress candidate had lent his support to the BJP candidate and was canvassing for "Pahari ekta" (Pahari unity) and voting for "winning Pahari candidate", recalls Singh.

Ratnesh Gupta reconfirms this. 'When Laxman Rawat, the Congress candidate, came for door-to-door contact programme, I saw him telling my guard to vote for "Pahari candidate"; he put his hand on my guard's shoulder and murmured something. Just then, people accompanying him told him that it was the house of an AAP leader. He quickly moved to the next house. I walked up to my guard and asked him, "What was he saying?" His reply was an eye-opener. "He asked me to vote for a Pahari candidate who is likely to win". It shocked me. The Congress candidate seemed to be implying to the Pahari voters to vote for the BJP candidate Ravinder Singh Negi', recalls Gupta.

Sheetal Singh says that he and his friends went to every mohalla in the constituency and realized that a similar message was being spread. 'It seems that Rawat, perhaps unsure of his win, was telling voters to vote for the BJP candidate in the name of Pahari ekta', says Sheetal, adding 'the RSS was also using its tested-and-trusted carpet bombing, by deploying its organizational local workers against Sisodia in his constituency. We also went to Sisodia's *padyatra*, which was quite impressive, but perhaps that was creating a smoke screen for Sisodia'. The former journalist adds, 'We got more clarity after talking to the person handling Sisodia's campaign. When we confronted him with the ground situation in local pockets, he did not have answers. It was clear that he was clueless, and Sisodia was in deep trouble. We passed on our feedback to the relevant people close to Sisodia'.

To make matters worse for Sisodia, the Opposition latched on to a comment he made in a TV debate. BJP's chief strategist Amit Shah had taken the reins of his party's campaign. At first, the party had tried to corner Kejriwal on his flagship programmes and schemes, but as that did not seem to be getting much traction with the voters, the BJP tried to corner the AAP on the CAA, which had been passed by Parliament while kicking up a political storm. The BJP-led coalition government claims that the CAA is necessary to speed up citizenship claims of religious minorities from Afghanistan, Bangladesh and Pakistan, all of which are India's neighbours and have a Muslim majority. Opponents of the Act claim that by fast-tracking citizenship for only minorities from these three countries, the law leaves out Muslims who could also be facing persecution and by singling out Muslims, the amendments violate India's Constitution which bans any discrimination on the basis of religion. The hugely contentious issue is currently before India's Supreme Court.

While the AAP had been one of the several parties which had opposed the amendments to the citizenship law in Parliament, it did not want to get drawn into the Hindu versus Muslim debate during the Delhi elections, preferring to keep the focus on development. While the issue at hand was whether the amendments were violative of the country's Constitution, on the ground it was being perceived by sections of the population as a Hindu–Muslim issue.

The BJP had tried to corner the AAP into a debate on the issue, but so far Kejriwal and his party had managed to steer clear. That changed on 23 January, when during an event organized by news channel News18 India, Sisodia was asked about the protests against the CAA and, in particular, the Shaheen Bagh blockade of one of the key arterial roads of the capital to its neighbouring city of Noida in UP.

Sisodia had replied, '*Manish Sisodia ke paas shayad Shaheen Bagh ka rasta nikaalne ka rasta na ho. Jiske paas hai aap usise poochhiye ki Shaheen Bagh ka rasta niklega to kaise niklega. Manish Sisodia ke paas Dilli ke school kholne ka rasta hai, mohalla clinic kholne ka rasta hai, bijli mein ho rahi chori rokkar bijli sasti karne ka rasta hai, aap uspar sawaal poochhiye. Shaheen Bagh ka rasta khulwaane ki jimmedaari meri nahin hai.* (Perhaps Manish Sisodia does not have the key to resolve the impasse at Shaheen Bagh. Ask those who have the key, how the way through Shaheen Bagh will be cleared. Sisodia knows how to set up schools and mohalla clinics, how to stop the theft of electricity and make it cheaper. You should go to the higher-ups and ask them the question of opening up the road through Shaheen Bagh, that is not my responsibility).'[16]

But the programme anchor Kishore Ajwani persisted, asking Sisodia to take a stand on the issue, to which he replied, 'I could be standing anywhere, I stand with the people of Shaheen Bagh.'

Sisodia had not said anything wrong and, if seen in the context of the larger question, it could be argued that Sisodia had put things in perspective. But it was just the kind of statement that the BJP had been hoping for. Within hours, the internet and the social media had been flooded with snippets taken from that interview. The clip of Sisodia saying 'I stand with the people of Shaheen Bagh' was used to make videos that made it seem as if Sisodia had endorsed 'anti-India' slogans and speeches made by some people associated with the Shaheen Bagh agitation.

While online trolls were doing their bit, the BJP latched on to the statement. From Amit Shah to a member of the Union Cabinet, they repeatedly referred to Sisodia's comments on Shaheen Bagh to hammer the AAP.

---

[16]Available at: https://www.youtube.com/watch?v=_r8ARRGXqCM, last accessed on 5 August 2020.

It was a double whammy for the AAP. Engaging with the BJP on the issue would further snowball it and set the momentum around it, while keeping quiet would signal accepting the allegations. The BJP, which had baited the AAP, now put its political machinery into high gear, using the statement by Kejriwal's second-in-command to corner both the CM and the AAP.

Faced with a tough decision, Kejriwal decided to sacrifice his most powerful figure—just like Bobby Fischer had surrendered his queen in the iconic 1956 game in New York.

Sisodia, second-in-command and one of the most visible talking heads of the party, was confined to his constituency by Kejriwal. Even in his constituency, Sisodia kept away from journalists. The BJP tried hard to keep the momentum going, using the Sisodia comment, but the issue did not make much impact as he was nowhere to be seen and the BJP was left with targeting him only in his own constituency.

'It must be a force of 10,000 to 12,000 people on the ground on a given day. They would be assigned pre-identified local chatter points to cover every single locality of the constituency. They would talk about this issue and share videos in the morning and would again check in the evening for the impact of the exercise, to ensure the communication along with the video clip had reached every single household and was creating the desired impact on target voter segment. It went on for several days,' says Sheetal Singh. 'It's typical RSS modus operandi. They don't believe in faces as much as depending on organizational strength and action. They had almost won the battle. The Congress candidate's hard campaigning in minority and Dalit localities was also eating into AAP's loyal vote bank,' he adds. 'By disengaging Sisodia from the campaign, Kejriwal made a smart move and managed to minimize the loss,' comments Singh.

On 11 February 2020, as the counting of votes progressed, trends indicated a landslide victory for the AAP. People were eagerly looking for trends on the seats that were considered difficult for the party or where a close contest had been predicted in opinion polls, but Sisodia's Patparganj was not among those.

The party headquarters at Rouse Avenue was flooded with volunteers from the city and other states. The drums seemed to be getting louder as it was becoming more and more apparent that the party was going to form the government again. Several of the volunteers had broken out in a song and dance.

But Kejriwal and many of the top leadership were nowhere to be seen. Kejriwal was inside his office with his lieutenants, closely monitoring TV channels and information coming in from party workers. There were a couple of key seats where the margin between AAP and BJP candidates kept fluctuating. In the end, Sisodia's seat still seemed to be hanging, while the other key contestants from the AAP seemed to be pulling through comfortably.

'What about Sisodia?' was one question all journalists were asking. A victory for the AAP was in the bag, but if Kejriwal's second-in-command Sisodia did not pull through, it would dent not only the celebrations but also Kejriwal's momentum.

'I knew at one in the afternoon that Sisodia would win,' Sanjay Singh, AAP's MP and the in-charge of the 2020 campaign for the party, tells us. Interestingly, Singh had been sticking to his claim of Sisodia's eventual victory on TV channels from the party office in Rouse Avenue even when the Deputy CM had been trailing. So, was this a lucky guess or a morale booster?

'Seats such as these depend a lot on strategy, last-minute booth management and alertness,' Singh says, before adding, 'We were monitoring the response in each booth where polling was taking place. We had realized that Sisodia needed to shore up his numbers and on polling day, we had asked his team to concentrate on getting the voters to come out and cast their vote, especially in specific areas where the contest was a close one.'

The Delhi election chief admits that a lot also depends on the day of the election and whether candidates and their teams can work to pull out the voters to cast their votes.

'One of our candidates got overconfident and even three hours before voting, we told him that he was running short by a thousand votes and he needed to focus on encouraging voters to come out. But the candidate was overconfident. As a result, he lost by 880 votes,' recalls Singh.

Most of these battles had gone AAP's way on the counting day, but that one crucial seat could have been the spoiler. There were only three last rounds of counting left and Sisodia was trailing by a margin of close to 1,700 votes. Giant TV screens put up by the party at its headquarters narrowed it down to Sisodia's seat. Several party workers could be seen with hands folded and heads bowed in prayer. These were the longest 30 minutes of the day. Finally, the news channels flashed: 'Sisodia wins by 3,207 votes'.

It was only then that Kejriwal, flanked by his wife and two children and accompanied by the party's leadership, emerged before the cameras at the party headquarters.

The drums played on for a long time that day in the AAP headquarters, long after even Kejriwal had left the balcony following his victory speech. Perhaps most of the hundreds of party workers who continued to dance on the lawns that day may not have realized just how close some of the political battles had been and what they had managed to do. The AAP had once again managed to beat Goliath in the 2020 elections.

10

THE ROAD AHEAD: OPENING THE FIELD TO BIGGER CHALLENGES

'Be it elections in the shadow of the Anti-cow Slaughter Agitation of 1966 or the demolition of Babri Masjid at Ayodhya in 1992, I can say with full authority and conviction that the 2020 Delhi elections were the most communal elections ever fought in the history of Independent India,' says Professor Abhay Kumar Dubey, a keen political observer.

According to Professor Dubey, the BJP appeared to have used a progressively graded strategy. In phase one, it shifted the entire narrative from issues such as the performance of the Kejriwal government in Delhi and local leadership of the challenger parties, to aggressive nationalism. In the second leg, it further moved the nationalism debate into a Hindu versus Muslim debate, and the third and the final leg of the strategy was to turn the elections into a battle, not between the BJP and the AAP, but between the Hindus and the Muslims.

Was the BJP using Delhi as a laboratory for its brand of politics, or did they actually not have a choice, as the party did not have much to offer by way of development? In either case, Professor Dubey believes that the BJP paid the price and saw that this aggressive communal campaign pitch didn't work and they are not likely to use it in future battles.

'Delhi was different,' he claims. The AAP had made it clear that it wanted to contest elections on the performance of its government in Delhi over the last five years. They had, right at the start, rolled out their campaign comparing the performance of the BJP-led municipal bodies with the work of the Kejriwal government in Delhi.

The BJP could not take that track, as the BJP-led municipal bodies had not done any work that the party could showcase in the Delhi elections. Their schools were in a shambles, lacking even the basic infrastructure such as desks and benches. The same was true about the hospitals and dispensaries run by the municipalities.

The common perception among voters was that the BJP-run municipalities were dens of corruption and mismanagement, and the AAP wasted no time in comparing the two models. On 9 January 2020, Kejriwal held a press conference and released a leaflet comparing the performance of the BJP-ruled municipal corporations and the work done by his government.[17]

Professor Dubey says, 'Local leadership of the BJP was corrupt and very uninspiring. Local leaders had done no work and they had wasted the opportunity. That made the fight tough for Amit Shah.'

The Clash of Models

Professor Dubey also attributes AAP's victory to the two different styles of development that the Modi and Kejriwal

---

[17]'BJP-ruled MCD "Most Corrupt Department", says Kejriwal,' *Outlook: The News Scroll*, 9 January 2020. Available at: https://www.outlookindia.com/newsscroll/bjpruled-mcd-most-corrupt-department-says-kejriwal/1704385, last accessed on 29 July 2020.

governments offered their electorates.

His belief is that the Modi government had a very popular development model which helped him shore up support from the poorest of the poor across the country. His schemes such as the Pradhan Mantri Jan-Dhan Yojana (PMJDY), Pradhan Mantri Ujjwala Yojna (PMUY), Ayushman Bharat Pradhan Mantri Jan Arogya Yojana (AB PM-JAY) and so on reached out to the most marginalized and economically backward sections of society.

The Ujjwala Yojna was officially launched by the PM in Balia (UP) on 1 May 2016. This scheme aimed to provide five crore LPG cooking gas connections to families below the poverty line (BPL) with a support of ₹1,600 per connection in the next three years. This was hugely popular, and the Modi government ensured that the beneficiaries were identified and the beneficiary data was effectively used for the following elections.

A similar story can be found about the 'Shauchalaya' or 'Izzat Ghar' scheme of constructing toilets and the 'Jan-Dhan' scheme of opening zero-balance savings bank accounts with added benefits. Despite hard criticism and often stinging attacks from the Opposition, Modi successfully created a bond with the poorest sections of the population and delivered benefits to them. Professor Dubey adds that schemes such as direct transfers of money to farmers and the Ayushman Bharat Yojna of healthcare benefits of up to ₹5 lakh fall in the same list. He says these pro-poor subsidy-based schemes helped Modi make his base among the poorest class of people in India.

But Professor Dubey feels that these schemes targeting the very poor were not customized for Delhi. Delhi's voters are not that poor, and most of them do not come under the ambit of these schemes. In Dubey's words, 'It was a fight between the two models. Kejriwal's model was customized for Delhi, Modi's model was not. Modi could not alter his model or schemes only for Delhi and paid the price. However, Kejriwal would encounter the same problem if his party were to step out of Delhi. He will have to study the issues of the new state and customize his model specifically for there. The AAP Delhi model, as it is today, will not sell everywhere.'

The Modi Model

The most interesting fact is that the Modi government's success in this outreach was made possible by the work done by its predecessor, the UPA government, in its second term in office. Under the social, economic and caste census, they had started the work of identifying the poorest households. The census had identified 10 crore of the most deprived households in India with precise identification details of name and addresses.[18] The Modi government used this data to implement its pro-poor schemes and to ensure these families were actually delivered the benefits.

The beneficiary data was used in elections: beneficiaries were not only identified, but the data was also provided to the state governments in the BJP-ruled states to organize PM

---

[18]The census was commissioned by the UPA government in 2011 and partial data was released in 2015 by the NDA government. Some of the data was released only later. The calculation of the most needy 10 crore households was on the basis of income per household. Please also see: Pranab Dhal Samanta, 'Will Yogi Adityanath March to the BJP's Beat of Class-based Political Insecurity?' *The Economic Times*, 21 March 2017. Available at: https://economictimes.indiatimes.com/blogs/et-commentary/will-yogi-adityanath-march-to-the-bjps-beat-of-class-based-political-insecurity/, last accessed on 6 August 2020.

Modi's rallies. Crores were reportedly spent on providing transport and logistics to these people to attend the PM's rallies, but the objective was achieved. These people voted for Modi in large numbers across caste lines. That was a defining development in contemporary Indian politics.

While Modi's campaign targeted the poorest and marginalized Indians, and delivered these schemes to the doorstep of the poorest man, the PM also made it a point to connect with that man, emotionally. In his speeches, Modi underlined how he was the author of the schemes, and wove personal stories around them. While talking about the Ujjwala scheme, he recalled how his mother cooked food on an earthen *chulha* (hearth) and how tears rolled down her cheeks because of the smoke coming from it. He said that he did not want other poor mothers of the country to go through the same unhealthy circumstances. Modi won the hearts of millions and an entirely new crop of voters who had never before voted for the BJP, were netted.

The communication strategy was carefully crafted, specifically targeting this new vote bank of 10 crore poor families. Modi talked about their pride and self-respect. He talked about their contribution and also the government's responsibility towards them. He reiterated his resolve to transform their lives and also gave a personal touch to these messages. The delivery of his schemes on the ground and the repeated communication were so compelling that they produced a strong bond with the target group.

The problem was that this model had no resonance with the voters of Delhi. The poorest of the poor targeted by Modi did not live in Delhi and this model did not benefit the city poor. The urban poor of Delhi had migrated from villages in UP, Bihar or other states and had come here with dreams in their eyes. They were not only making a viable living for themselves in the city, but also earning enough to provide for their extended families back in the village.

For the Delhi migrant, the rules of these schemes bypassed them, either because they were earning more than the minimum allowed to avail the benefits, or were excluded as beneficiaries because they had some basic facilities such as a telephone connection or a two-wheeler or refrigerator in their homes.

'If we look at Kejriwal's journey in Delhi, it becomes clear that he thoroughly studied the issues being faced by Delhiites and prepared his political programme around that. Do you remember his iconic photograph where he is restoring electricity connections which had been cut off for non-payment of dues? The people of Delhi were fed up with the rising electricity tariff. It was an issue close to their heart and here was the CM personally giving redressal to the issue. Kejriwal, an anti-corruption crusader, soon picked up the issue and shook the Congress and the BJP from their hold on the people and made a space for himself,' points out Professor Dubey.

In its debut election (2013), the AAP won 28 out of 70 seats and changed the political landscape of the national capital forever. However, Kejriwal did not stop there. After his party's landslide victory in the 2015 elections, Kejriwal very carefully created a model of governance which provided affordable living to the urban poor, his ardent supporter class. He created a uniform appeal for himself as a leader who cared for his people. And just like the Modi model, Kejriwal also connected with the common man, raising their aspirations by delivering on the basics of education, healthcare, electricity and water.

The Delhi Model

Delhi's Finance and Education Minister, Sisodia expands on the Delhi model of development that built a solid rapport with AAP voters.

Drawing a circle on the table of a Connaught Place (CP) Outer Circle restaurant on a hot and humid afternoon, Sisodia says, 'It's a circle.' Sisodia, Kejriwal's close aide from his Parivartan days, is considered to be the chief architect of the Delhi model of governance. He is not only credited with revolutionary transformation in the education sector, but has also earned plaudits for an economic turnaround of the city government.

'It's a circle of happiness and prosperity. It's very simple. All you have to do as a government is to facilitate your businessmen. They help you generate revenue. This revenue helps you with resources to run social schemes, which in turn help the average citizen to save money—money that they used to spend on availing basic services from the government, such as water, electricity and so on,' says Sisodia.

'With this saving in his pocket, he goes back to the market and spends it. He refuels your economy and you see your economy skyrocketing,' he grins as he gestures with his right hand, with a fork in it, of an airplane taking off. 'That's no rocket science,' he adds. Dressed in a half-sleeved shirt and casual trousers, Delhi's Deputy CM, Education Minister and Finance Minister Sisodia was a surprise guest at the restaurant that late afternoon as the staff was about to wind up the first half of the day's business. After the selfie session with restaurant staff got over, we settled down for a late lunch as the only customers in the first-floor dining space.

'Show us the magic wand that helped an inexperienced set

of people win laurels from the likes of former UN Secretary General Ban Ki-moon, His Holiness the Dalai Lama and A.P.J. Abdul Kalam,' we asked jocularly. Eyes sparkling with confidence, he immediately responded with a grin, 'It's honest politics.'

Sisodia says that when they came to power, there was apprehension among bureaucrats about what the future would inevitably hold. They thought that the new government would start corrupt practices in five or six months, taking money for transfers and postings as they eventually succumbed to pressure. Everyone expected that the emphasis on transparency and clean politics would go up in smoke very soon.

In a few months, they realized that these were a different type of people. A very senior bureaucrat came to Sisodia and said that the best thing about the AAP government was that the bureaucrats did not have to worry about strings of corruption attached to the instructions coming from the political leadership. He said that they were so used to this in the past, that 'whenever a direction came from the ministers, we were in the habit of scrutinizing it for the financial interests of the minister in the direction. Now, we don't have to worry about this. We still scrutinize the directions to see how they can be implemented within the boundaries of the law and precedents. That's our job, but we don't have to be unnecessarily worried about potential corruption,' the bureaucrat had told Sisodia.

'That was a huge informal compliment for our style of government and provided a very necessary feedback to show us we were going the right way,' says Sisodia. 'When you do honest politics, you are surrounded by clean-hearted and honest professionals. When you become dishonest, you are surrounded by dishonest people who look for an opportunity to grab a contract, an opportunity to get kickbacks. These people would look for an opportunity to hike electricity tariffs to make money. And when you do honest politics, people approach you with ideas to help you slash electricity bills. That's the secret.'

'Clean intentions are one thing, but then where does the money come from?' we asked.

'There is no dearth of money if you want to do good work,' retorts Sisodia. He goes on to explain, 'The first thing in politics is to understand the needs of the people. Once you understand their needs, you will find experts on economy, education or health. The main thing is whether you understand the pain and problems of your constituents or not, whether you are committed to address those issues or not.'

He gives a very interesting example of the importance of listening to people. When they first came to power in 2013, the tax rate was largely 12.5 per cent on most of the goods.[19] In the rest of the country, it was between 13 and 14 per cent. There was a lot of pressure from the Union Finance Ministry and other states as well, for Delhi to rationalize the tax rates and raise them up to around 14 per cent. The AAP government also needed money to launch welfare schemes that they had promised. They held consultations with traders, and they proved to be a real eye-opener. The traders said that if you

---

[19]Technical Guide to Delhi VAT, The Institute of Chartered Accountants of India, New Delhi, Page 19. Available at: http://idtc-icai.s3.amazonaws.com/download/Delhi-VAT.pdf, last accessed on 6 August 2020.
General Scheme of the Delhi VAT Act. A dealer is liable to pay tax at the prescribed rates on every sale of goods effected by him. The goods are taxed at the following rates:
- (i) Goods specified in the first schedule: Nil
- (ii) Goods specified in the second schedule: 1%
- (iii) Goods specified in the third schedule: 5%
- (iv) Goods specified in the fourth schedule: 12.5% to 30%
- (v) Unspecified goods: 12.50%

retained the tax rate of 12.5 per cent or above, people will try to evade paying tax and would trade goods without bills from the traders. But if the tax rates are slashed to 5 per cent, traders would help to enforce the tax. They assured the government that even by reducing the tax rate so drastically, the tax mop up would not shrink.

The AAP government decided to go for this experiment and started by slashing the tax slab on timber to a mere 5 per cent from 12.5 per cent during its second term, in August 2015. The results were astonishing. The tax mop up for the year 2015–16 went up, compared to the preceding year. After the success of this experiment, they slashed the tax rate on another 44 items from 12.5 per cent to 5 per cent. It gave a great advantage to the traders of Delhi and their businesses saw a sudden surge. The government revenue mop up also shot up.

The second important decision was to stop the Inspector Raj. 'When we took over, there was rampant Inspector Raj or "raid raj". The value added tax (VAT) inspectors would visit traders on one pretext or the other. We stopped this practice. We told them to go for surveys or raids only on the basis of data-based evidence. VAT raids completely stopped and this instilled a further confidence in traders,' Sisodia said.

'These tax departments are considered to be the most corrupt organs of the government. Did you feel resistance from the bureaucracy when you put a stop to arbitrary raids?' I asked.

'No! There was not much resistance,' Sisodia replied. 'And there was a reason behind it. During the raid raj days, postings with raid-authorizing powers were sold by politicians. The bureaucrat bidding the highest would get the posting. That was the norm. When we came to power, we posted the best and honest officers. This bidding system was stopped. The message to the bureaucrats was clear. Since you don't have to pay for good postings, you also stop corruption. It worked,' he adds.

'If you look at the parallel data, you will realize that it's not a "pat your back" account of a finance minister. When the country's economy is going downhill, and it has been so since 2017 with no signs of revival, when state GDPs are touching new lows, Delhi's economy is showing buoyancy. The budget has doubled; it has gone up from ₹30,000 crore (during 2014–15) to ₹60,000 crore (in 2019–20). In 2019–20, Delhi's per capita income was three times the national average. These numbers show the robustness of the Delhi economy. What is it if not the impact of our model of economy?' asks Sisodia with pride, putting forth the evidence.

'What I am saying can be corroborated by evidence. In the month of September last year, when we implemented the free bus ride scheme for ladies, Satyender Jain and I were waiting for someone near Delhi Zoo. Two girls came up to us and thanked us for the free bus ride scheme for ladies. They told us that they lived in Narela and worked in Gurgaon for ₹20,000 a month. They used to spend ₹3,000 every month on bus fare. They told us that with this new scheme, they would now save this money, which was a good savings account. To celebrate this saving, they had brought their parents for a visit to the zoo. This was evidence that savings become disposable income, which returns to the market to refuel it. These savings give a boost to the market.'

Another example is from Sisodia's constituency, Patparganj. He was making a round of his constituency, when a shopkeeper of a small electrical shop came up to greet him. It was after the government had implemented the 'lifeline electricity scheme' under which no bill was to be paid for electricity consumption of up to 200 units. He thanked Sisodia, who thought that the man was happy for this direct saving, but he had a different story to tell. The shopkeeper said that his business had been passing through a rough patch, as there were no buyers in the market. He said, 'After the free electricity scheme was launched, people in large numbers started getting zero electricity bills. Now, they are coming to my shop to buy electrical items with these savings. I am getting back my customers.'

'That was another evidence of how these measures, which are often mocked by our political opponents as "freebies", are actually economy boosters. This is what Nobel laureate Abhijit Banerjee says. Delhi is a laboratory where Banerjee's theory has been proved to be correct,' tells a proud Sisodia.

'These are numbers, but what does the Delhi model mean for a common man?' we ask Sisodia.

'It is simple. Our job is to instill this confidence in the mind and heart of the common man of Delhi that if a child is born in the family, he doesn't need to worry about quality education. He should be confident that the government will ensure the child gets quality education. Similarly about healthcare; he should have the confidence that he doesn't have to worry for his ageing parents' medical expenses. He should be confident of getting affordable and quality healthcare. He should be confident that he will be able to afford the electricity bill with his income from his business or salary.

'If we succeed in instilling this confidence in the heart and mind of an average Delhiite, I think our job is done. And that is what our Delhi model means to a common man,' tells Sisodia.

As the man in charge of the finances, was he ever worried? Sisodia says that while making the first Budget, he was very worried that they were taking a huge risk by spending so much on education. Close to 24 per cent of the entire budget of ₹41,129 crore was being spent on education, followed by ₹4,787 crore on the health sector. Those who understood traditional politics or who were following the system, while agreeing to spend more on education and healthcare, strongly advised against spending so much on education right in the beginning.

But, the question is, what next? Can the AAP win elections with this model alone? Will people vote for education and healthcare in this country? These are big questions that have been staring at the leadership of the political start-up.

'Delhi has put forth the evidence,' a confident Sisodia asserts and corroborates his argument with facts. 'Before 2013, there was a huge question if the people of this country would ever vote on the issue of corruption. It was unthinkable till then that a party would come up and promise to deliver clean politics and honest government and people would vote on this issue. Then, the 2013 and 2015 Delhi assembly elections were contested totally on the issue of corruption.

'So when we doubt if the people will ever vote on issues such as clean and honest government, education, healthcare, water, electricity, etc., we doubt their intelligence. When they find a credible alternative, they vote for it. In Delhi, they did not vote for the BJP or the Congress. They voted for the AAP. Then again, in 2020, the elections happened totally on the performance of the AAP government. Education and healthcare were big issues. So, these two elections have completely debunked the myth that people don't vote on these issues.'

The question then is: what next for the AAP government? What are their ambitions of growing beyond Delhi? When they try to move to other places, will they be able to sell this model across the country?

'We do not have to sell this model. The people of Delhi will sell the model. It is one thing for me to tell people in another state that our party is the best. But when people from Delhi talk to people in other states that in Delhi they have the cheapest electricity in all of India, and that many people get zero electricity bills, they are our best advocates and have sold our model. People will demand that if this has been done in Delhi, they too want the AAP to come and give them development on the same model,' says Sisodia.

If the next general election is held on the question of 'if not the ruling party, then who?' where would the AAP be? Can they provide a viable option, being such a small party with relatively limited resources? Can they make a mark on the entire country on the basis of its development model?

Sisodia says, 'Our dream is not that the party should make a mark in the entire country. Our dream is that this idea of good governance should leave its footprint in the whole country. If people start to demand good governance in all the states of the country, then all the people, social workers, government, all will have to come forward. We would all have to work for it.'

Today, many state governments and politicians from other states are flocking to Delhi to see its model schools and mohalla clinics. Representatives of two main parties from all states have come to study the Delhi government school model, and to learn about the Happiness Curriculum. Several states such as Assam and Jharkhand have already started mohalla clinics. In Jharkhand, the mohalla clinics have been renamed 'Atal clinics'. People from across the world are also coming to see the Delhi government, and school education ministers of 12 states have come to Delhi to study the education model, while the CMs of Jharkhand and Maharashtra have also shown a lot of interest. The exciting work being done in Delhi is being discussed in other states and there is pressure on their leaders to deliver. Whether the governments there will adopt these, only time will tell.

We ask Sisodia whether the AAP plans to make a national foray again and try to be part of a national government at the Centre.

'The country needs us to serve the people. If electricity, water, healthcare and education become the issues demanded by the electorate, then our party is the only option, and there is no alternative. It would take time to create this larger picture to achieve this', Sisodia declares.

Moving Beyond the Capital

AAP leader Atishi Singh asserts that for the AAP, it is imperative that they do expand to other parts of the country in the future.

Singh, a member of AAP's Political Affairs Committee and National Executive Advisor to Deputy CM Sisodia, was also a key member of the party's manifesto drafting committee for the 2013 assembly elections. Singh got her second master's degree in Education Research from the University of Oxford as a Rhodes Scholar. She put this to use to help revamp the state of government schools in the national capital. In 2019, Singh had run for the East Delhi constituency but was trumped by the BJP, which took all of the seven Lok Sabha seats in Delhi. A year later, however, she contested and won the Kalkaji assembly seat in Delhi.

So, what according to her are the biggest accomplishments of the AAP government on which the people voted the party back to power?

According to Singh, their party's biggest achievement was to provide people with evidence that honest and people-centric politics are viable; that politics can happen without criminals, dynasts and the corrupt; that a party can win elections while speaking the language of unity and harmony, rather than of divisive rule and that good governance performance on education, healthcare, water and electricity can be electorally rewarding.

'This is a spectacular achievement as it foundationally challenges the decades-old identity politics and shifts it to citizenship-based politics. This is a new form of politics. When the history of Indian politics is written, AAP's contribution will stand out,' she says.

She feels that people voted the AAP to power for many reasons. One was electricity, when they had slashed electricity bills by half, and then not raised them for five years. 'Rather than provide 200 units of free electricity to all, we helped to provide relief to the common people, particularly those hit by the pain caused by joblessness and rising inflation. People voted for us because they saw that we truly care for them,' she says.

'People voted us to power because their children told them stories of better teaching and learning in the classrooms, and then saw with their own eyes, the huge transformation of the schools. For the first time, they experienced a government that treated them with dignity, and was at par with those whose children attend private schools.

'People voted for us because they could now avail of free medicines and medical tests within walking distance of their homes. They felt cared for, particularly the elderly and the women, whose health needs had remained most neglected till now.

'Above all, people voted for us because they saw in Kejriwal a leader who spoke their language, fought for their rights and delivered for their better future,' says Singh.

A lot has however happened since 2013. While admitting that the party has come a long way, we ask Singh if she feels that the AAP has matured and to explain how it has changed.

'The most spectacular change is the increasing dominance of social media platforms. With internet penetration increasing substantially since then, and social media being accessible to crores of Indians, it has emerged as a potent tool for every party,' according to Singh.

She says that the AAP, in her view, is in many ways still the same party that fought the 2013 elections—driven by idealism and committed to India, people's welfare and transparency in public governance. 'It is still the party of selfless volunteers who are stubborn about transforming India,' says Singh.

'Yet, in some sense, we are now a different party. Back then, we talked of a dream—a dream of corruption-free governance, a dream of functional public schools and hospitals, and people-centric governance. When we announced a 50 per cent subsidy for electricity bills, people ridiculed us. When we promised free water in 2013 and then again in 2015, the media mocked us. The earlier government had been pushing for privatization of water supply and there were several parts of the capital which were considered as 'dry zone', where there was no or negligible government supply of water. The belief was that this was going to be a scheme only on paper, as it was not possible to supply water to these areas and even if that could be done, it would come at a very high cost. Even when we committed to transforming government schools, we met with indifference and hopelessness.

'But now we have proved that the dream is a possibility and, in fact, a reality. And now we are saying all of India can be very different. We can all live in a healthy, educated, peaceful and loving country. The only change needed is in its politics,' she adds.

So, if politics needs to change, what about the political

leaders themselves? We ask Singh what changes she sees in herself.

'A transition from an academic to a public person and now a lawmaker,' she responds. 'True change is possible only through people's politics. When the rules of the game are rigged, there is little or no value in small changes you make as an academic. The radical change comes from people's power.' She feels that this is what the AAP demonstrated through their last five years of extraordinary work in sectors such as education, health, water and electricity. She adds, 'My own journey has humbled me as I witnessed ordinary people turn heroes at the drop of a hat, and the selflessness of our volunteers who staked everything they have in the hope of a better India. Their courage has made me a much more courageous person and made my inner moral compass stronger.'

Speaking of the 2020 elections, she says that she is truly humbled by the infinite faith of the people of Kalkaji, who gave her unflinching support. 'I never felt like I was contesting the elections, but that the thousands of people in Kalkaji were. I am immensely grateful to all of them. Our campaign was focused on our past work, and future action plan. Contrary to our earlier campaign, where I was practically contesting against Modi in whose name the BJP polled votes, we connected with people better, and got our message across sharper.'

Almost all parties are born out of a struggle or a movement to offer better alternatives than the existing ones. So, as the AAP becomes more politically savvy, is there a danger that it too will become just like the other parties who follow politics of convenience?

Singh vehemently denies this and says, 'The AAP is not an ordinary party; it was born out of the immense struggle of ordinary people out there to transform our country, and we won't stop unless that dream is achieved. It is this hope and dream that give us strength. False cases are slapped on us, our offices are raided, our volunteers beaten and yet, the AAP continues to lead the way, because truth and honesty are powerful. We have time and again stood for our beliefs, even at the cost of being marginalized. We will continue to do so even at great personal risks.'

She reiterates that the AAP politics is the politics of people's daily lives and is rooted in their welfare with particular focus on education, healthcare, water, electricity and transportation, and that the AAP governance record is being appreciated even by their strongest critics. She emphasizes that their party acknowledges the historical discrimination of women, Dalits, Muslims and transgenders, and that 'unlike other parties whose sole objective is to grab power by means of playing divide and rule, our goal remains social justice and social cohesion.'

She says that the AAP is powered by the energy of lakhs of selfless volunteers across India and outside, and the leadership, vision and courage of Kejriwal. 'With these two forces, the AAP is becoming the true voice of ordinary people,' she adds.

So, is it finally time for the AAP to make a significant dent on the national stage? We ask Singh about her vision for the party and how aggressively she thinks the party should look to expand and go national, given that its earlier attempts to do so had not been very successful and in the 2019 Lok Sabha elections, its earlier four Lok Sabha seats had reduced to one. Should the AAP be even daring to think of such a move?

Singh is very clear-sighted and emphatic on this issue. She articulates her vision for the country and for AAP's important role in the future of the country. 'Some fights are not fought only when you are assured of the victory. They are fought because that's the right thing to do. And that's what we did.

And we will do it over and over again.

'Our country is being ruled by a political party that is hell-bent on destroying every democratic institution, that does not care about people's pain caused by joblessness and poor governance performance, and a party that considers Muslims and Dalits to be second-grade citizens. It is being fuelled by a hatred-driven propaganda machinery of the paid media.

'We, on the contrary, believe in an India where all have decent jobs, children study in good schools, have access to quality healthcare, and there is love and cohesion in our society. It is this dream we are fighting for. In fact, everyone should join this fight. It is their fight too,' she adds.

The decision for the AAP to go national was based on this thought. 'Our spectacular governance performance ensured our resounding victory in the recent elections. Within 24 hours, nearly 11 lakh people expressed their willingness to join the party.

'Lakhs of people from Bihar, UP, Haryana and Maharashtra are sick and tired of politics as usual and yearning for a change. It is this voice and aspiration of people that we are responding to. As a result, we are the principal opposition party in Punjab, state party in Goa having secured more than 6 per cent vote share, and now have footprints in several panchayat and urban local bodies as well as university union posts. A decent performance in one more state, and we will become a national party. What does it say about a less than eight-year-old political party?' she challenges.

So, how does the AAP expand and what according to Singh are the big challenges for the party over the next few years?

'The economy has only gotten worse for the past several years,' she notes. 'India has recorded one of the highest levels of unemployment since the 1970s, the GDP growth rate shrank to around 4 per cent, foreign investment dried up and the powerful nexus of some businesses with the top politicians in our country has made it unviable for business growth overall. At the same time, the performance of the average public schools continued to be dismal.'

Singh says that this was even before the COVID-19 pandemic hit the country. 'The current pandemic and its outcomes have also exposed the crumbling public health infrastructure as well. Crores of people have fallen into poverty as a result of a thoughtless lockdown that showed no sign of planning. It became one of the world's largest displacement exercises. Visuals of elderly women and their children walking hundreds of kilometres shocked everyone's conscience,' says Singh.

Singh says that the AAP plans to continue focusing on ordinary people and 'highlighting their struggles. We will continue to tell their stories of pain till it is redressed. We will mobilize people at the grassroots in all parts of the country and become a force to reckon with.'

She also chalks out the party's plans for expanding in other states. 'Our immediate focus will be to provide alternative politics in Punjab and Goa as the people there have become sick of the politics of the BJP and the Congress. We also plan to consolidate in UP, Bihar and Maharashtra,' she says with a fire in her eyes.

The Troubleshooter

After having won a fiercely fought battle for the capital in February, there was little time to celebrate. Barely 12 days after the election results, riots broke out in North-East Delhi, the worst the capital has seen since the 1984 anti-Sikh riots that followed the assassination of the then PM Indira Gandhi by her Sikh bodyguards. The AAP government was put to the test by these riots. While AAP's critics and even several supporters say that the party has been largely silent on the riots, only appealing for calm, Rajya Sabha MP and Delhi election in-charge, Sanjay Singh has been the exception and accused the BJP of engineering the riots as part of 'deep-rooted conspiracy', a charge Singh repeated at a press conference on 20 July.[20]

Singh's allegations come amid a tussle between the Lt Governor of Delhi, Anil Baijal, and the AAP government over the appointment of special prosecutors to handle the Delhi riot cases. Baijal had appointed six special prosecutors recommended by the police. Singh, who had accused the Delhi Police of not doing enough to try and stop the violence and of not properly conducting investigations or filing charges against some of the rioters, has maintained that the latest appointments are aimed at shielding the truth about the riots from coming out.

Two months earlier, Singh spoke to us: 'After the Lok Sabha elections, we (the AAP) realized that we should focus on Delhi and the work we had done in Delhi. We realized that the BJP would try and trap us. They would try and communalize the elections. That is why Kejriwal held several press conferences to inform the people.'

As a founding member of the AAP and member of the party's powerful Political Affairs Committee, Singh is among AAP's top political strategists and troubleshooters.

---

[20]Sourav Roy Barman, 'As AAP Insists on Lawyers, It Says: BJP Engineered Riots in Delhi,' *The Indian Express*, 20 July 2020. Available at: https://indianexpress.com/article/india/delhi-riots-aap-delhi-sanjay-singh-6514008/, last accessed on 29 July 2020.

We asked him if it was fair to say that the AAP and Kejriwal had not done enough or not seen enough on the streets of Delhi to try and contain the riots and ask for calm.

'In which state does the CM go on the ground at the time of riots? Will the police control the riots or secure the CM? No, this does not happen anywhere. In Bhadrak (Odisha), did Naveen Patnaik (Odisha CM) go there when riots happened in 2017?[21] The fact is that during riots, a responsible person should not go there and divert attention. The police need to be given a free hand to quell the violence and if the police is not working, then to administer that.'

Singh says that he will continue to raise the issue of lack of fairness by the Delhi Police in filing charge sheets in the Delhi riots cases. We ask him how he sees the future and what comes next for the AAP.

'We will have to create our organization across the country and that will determine which elections we can fight. This victory will help in organization building. It is also a big signal that elections can be fought on development and won on development, especially when the counter is communal,' says Singh.

'Every party wants to grow, but it cannot do so at a fast rate all the time. Even the BJP has had its ups and downs. The Congress has never come back to power in UP since 1989, it has had a 30-year *vanvaas*.' Singh adds, 'It's not possible to predict the growth chart of any party: the AAP has its footprint across the country, somewhere it's more, some places, it's less.

---

[21]Debabrata Mohanty, 'Odisha: Bhadrak Communal Violence Has Taken Many by Surprise,' *The Indian Express*, 12 April 2017. Available at: https://indianexpress.com/article/india/odisha-bhadrak-communal-violence-has-taken-many-by-surprise-curfew-facebook-god-comment-hindu-muslim-4610171/, last accessed on 29 July 2020.

You will find AAP people from Goa to the Andamans, Kashmir to Kanyakumari. So, we have a footprint everywhere.'

Is the AAP falling into the same problem like some of the regional parties which are built around a single popular leader? Can other leaders emerge, especially if the AAP plans to grow?

'Leaders did emerge. Even in Punjab, leaders emerged; in other states, leaders will emerge, that is for sure. We will only contest where we believe we have a chance of winning. We will not fight elections for the sake of fighting elections. We learnt this lesson in 2014,' answers Singh.

'A week is a long time in politics,' Singh tells us, quoting British PM Sir Harold Wilson. 'So what may happen, when it may happen, one cannot say; after all, like demonetization, could anyone have predicted that?'

The Architect

'To the victor go the spoils' or so the saying goes. Kejriwal, once self-proclaimed anarchist and now three-time CM, may not have had much time to go over the spoils since the 2020 election results were announced. For shortly after his party's impressive victory in Delhi, riots took place in the capital and barely a month after that, a national lockdown was announced by the central government. When restrictions were relaxed, Delhi emerged as one of the hotspots for COVID-19 cases, stretching the city's medical infrastructure to the limit.

With the government giving its full attention to tackling the pandemic in Delhi, it was a real challenge to pin down Kejriwal for an interview for this book. While there had been several quick words and thoughts exchanged, it was only in the third week of July that we got a little time to speak with the architect of the AAP.

We asked Kejriwal to share his insights on what made the difference in the 2020 elections.

'For two crore Delhiites, the last five years have been a journey from pain to relief. The electricity had become unaffordable. The electricity bills were eating into the money meant for providing food to the family, for providing medicines and medical treatment to the family. The money saved to buy home appliances would often go to the power company as the electricity bill. We understood this pain of the common people and reduced the electricity bills to half. Electricity tariff was not raised in five years and rather, we provided 200 units of lifeline electricity for free,' says Kejriwal. Like his party colleagues, Kejriwal says that the real success of the party has been in delivering on the promises made to the people, be it electricity, drinking water, healthcare or education.

'I think a dream was being realized in the lives of more than 19 million people in Delhi. After decades of neglect, some real work had started. And a very beautiful picture of the Delhi of their dreams was emerging—of world-class schools, of mohalla clinics and world-class hospitals; a Delhi where there were no power cuts. It was not my dream alone, it was a shared dream of the two crore people of Delhi,' says Kejriwal. 'The BJP tried to shift the narrative to hatred and polarization on communal lines, but the people of Delhi saw it as a disruption of their dream. They felt threatened. They had seen how the BJP-run municipal bodies had turned into dens of corruption and misgovernance. They had seen how the BJP-ruled MCDs had turned Delhi into a heap of garbage. They abhorred the sight of the ever-rising mountains of garbage created by the BJP-run municipal corporations of Delhi. They felt protective of their dream of making Delhi a truly world-class city.'

According to Kejriwal, the AAP should also be thankful to

the people who ran a poisonous political campaign and lost the elections miserably. They ended up helping the people of Delhi send a message to the social activists, small political activist groups and parties in power in other states, that good work in transforming people's lives through development, healthcare and education can be politically rewarding. He says, 'Decades-old identity and formula politics of divide and rule can be decisively defeated and buried through people-centric politics of development.' That was the clear message from the 2020 elections.

'I think these elections will have historic relevance because the voters of Delhi have busted the myth that formula politics cannot be defeated and development can never make you win elections. It's a historic contribution of the people of Delhi to India's democracy and it will inspire young politicians to say goodbye to politics of caste and religion, of divide and rule and embrace a new brand of politics which is people-centric,' says Kejriwal, emphatically.

How has politics personally changed Kejriwal, over the years?

Kejriwal says that the change has been both overwhelming and humbling. 'When we started this journey, I had never imagined that so many people will give me so much space in their lives, that they will give me so much space in their hearts.'

Becoming emotional about his interactions with the people, Kejriwal added, 'We spend most of our time among our people. When I go and meet them, they hold my hands, they hug me, elders hug me tight and pat my back, old women often take my face in their hands and kiss my head or my forehead, young children often touch my feet and show their school report cards to me with pride. Often, people become speechless and tears roll down their cheeks. These moments touch my soul. These moments give me tremendous strength to fight for the India of our dreams. This has changed me completely. The people of Delhi have become my family.'

Laughing, he adds, 'When we had started this journey, we were often accused of ignoring our families, and now I have become a man thinking of his family all the time.'

So, how sure was he that several of the schemes such as free water and electricity will take off and be sustainable?

'Honestly speaking, even some of us were not sure whether the steps we had proposed would actually deliver the results. Be it huge allocation of funds for education and healthcare, or rejuvenating the economy by making disposable money available to the common man and facilitating our traders, our experiments have borne fruit. We have shown that honest politics is the only answer.

'Even while giving relief to our people on electricity and water, while giving free bus rides to our sisters and free pilgrimage to our elders, we have become a surplus economy. Our budget size has doubled from ₹30,000 crore to ₹60,000 crore, Delhi's per capita income today is three times the national average. Jal Board revenues have increased by 51 per cent in five years while giving 20,000 litres of free water to every family in Delhi. So today, we are confident and experienced people with a very successful Delhi model of governance to showcase,' says Kejriwal.

So, what about a bigger role for the AAP, beyond Delhi? How did he see Delhi's verdict and what was the next big idea for the AAP?

Kejriwal says that he sees a twofold role for the AAP. Its victory in Delhi has inspired millions of youth who aspire to bring about change, who want to serve their country. 'In less than 24 hours of the announcement of the Delhi election results, more than 11 lakh people registered with the AAP to join the mission to transform our country. Most of them are young people from UP, Bihar, Punjab, Maharashtra and other states,' he says.

'This victory has made them believe that change is possible. We can break the status quo and help India usher in a new era of development. We will take this torch of hope to every street, every mohalla of our country. We will awaken the people and make them believe that change is possible, it only needs you,' says Kejriwal, 'The Delhi elections have shown that dividing people on religious or caste lines will not work. If politicians learn this lesson, the country will be transformed sooner than we think.'

The second ray of hope according to Kejriwal comes from the fact that the 'stories of AAP's work happening in Delhi have reached every nook and corner of the country. Be it mohalla clinics or Delhi's government schools, people are talking about Delhi's success stories everywhere. That is the reason why almost every state government in the country has sent its officers to study the Delhi model. Education ministers of 12 states have visited Delhi to visit our schools and to understand how our education model works. So, the pressure for good governance and honest politics is building up on politicians and political parties.'

∽

INDEX